P9-DOF-181

A Student's Guide to IRISH AMERICAN Genealogy

Oryx American Family Tree Series

A Student's Guide to
IRISH AMERICAN
Genealogy

By Erin McKenna

Oryx Press
1996

NEW HANOVER COUNTY
PUBLIC LIBRARY
201 CHESTNUT STREET
WILMINGTON, N C 28401

Copyright 1996 by The Rosen Publishing Group, Inc.
Published in 1996 by The Oryx Press
4041 North Central at Indian School Road
Phoenix, Arizona 85012-3397

All rights reserved. No part of this publication may be reproduced
or transmitted in any form or by any means, electronic or mechan-
ical, including photocopying, recording, or by any information
storage and retrieval system, without permission in writing
from The Oryx Press.

Printed and bound in the United States of America.

∞ The paper used in this publication meets the minimum
requirements of American National Standard for Information
Science—Permanence of Paper for Printed Library Materials,
ANSI Z39.48, 1984.

Library of Congress Cataloging-in-Publication Data
McKenna, Erin.
   A student's guide to Irish American genealogy / Erin McKenna.
      p.   cm. — (Oryx American family tree series)
   Includes bibliographical references (p.   ) and index.
   Summary: A guide to genealogical research in the United States and
Ireland for Irish Americans. Includes information on the history of
Irish immigration.
   ISBN 0-89774-976-6
   1. Irish Americans—Genealogy—Handbooks, manuals, etc.
2. Irish Americans—Bibliography. [1. Irish Americans—Genealogy—
Handbooks, manuals, etc. 2. Irish Americans—Bibliography.]
I. Title. II. Series.
E184.I6M37   1996
016.973′049162—dc20   96-26070
                                                          CIP
                                                          AC

Contents

Chapter 4. Researching in Ireland, 106

A pioneer in the male-dominated world of art, Georgia O'Keeffe was at the vanguard of American modernism. She often incorporated the landscape and architecture of New Mexico in her paintings. O'Keeffe's father was a native of Ireland who had immigrated to Wisconsin.

Chapter 1
Your Irish American Heritage

What does it mean to be an Irish American? Is it the big St. Patrick's Day parade on Fifth Avenue in New York City? Is it eating corned beef and cabbage? Is it wearing an Aran sweater or a green scarf? These may all be outward expressions of your heritage. But the search for your Irish roots starts with you and your interest in learning more about the contributions that your parents, grandparents, and great-grandparents made to the United States. You may be curious to learn why your ancestors left, how they traveled, and where in Ireland they came from. These questions will lead to more questions and, with some luck and good research, you will begin to gather facts, analyze the information, and take those first steps to learning more about your family and your Irish American heritage.

Why Trace Your Irish Roots?

When you visited your grandmother's house, do you remember the pictures she had in special places or those mementos she never let anyone touch? Perhaps one day you asked her about the photo of the young man in the funny, old-fashioned uniform. She began to talk about her mother's brother Willie, who went into the army and served in World War I. When you asked her more about Uncle Willie, she said simply, "He died in France and is buried there." The picture was one of her mother's greatest treasures. She then picked up a picture of two young girls about ages five and seven and started talking about having the picture taken with her older sister. Suddenly, you realized that this little girl was your grandmother. The next picture you saw was of two scruffy-looking people with long hair dressed in bell-bottomed jeans and tie-dyed T-shirts. "Who are they?" you asked, and she told you that it was your Dad and his sister, Aunt Mary, when they were in high school. This attire was quite different from the clothes your Dad wears today.

Then she showed you the seashell from her first trip to the beach, the music box your grandfather gave her, and the bracelet her grandmother gave her on her sixteenth birthday. These are no longer just objects—they are links to your family history. The more you talk with your grandmother and other relatives, the more you will learn about your family and the puzzle we call genealogy.

Genealogists, or family historians, are people who are searching for clues that will provide information and documentation about their ancestors' lives. There are many different types of tools that can be used for this work. Family stories and traditions are part of the picture. They contain some of the clues that will lead you to more official documentation. Libraries, archives, and vital records provide the documentation that you will need to gather to verify family stories. This is a little like being a detective—you will need to listen, read, and analyze all the available information, and then verify that your conclusions are right. Let's start learning how to become a family history detective. Your first task will be to gain a fuller appreciation and understanding of the land of your ancestors and the reasons why they chose to leave Ireland. This knowledge can serve as the backdrop to your research on your own family.

Tracing Your Roots If You Are Adopted

If you are adopted and do not know the identities of your birth parents, you may wonder whether any of the techniques in this book will apply to you. The answer is yes. If your adoptive family is Irish American, there is no reason why you cannot use the techniques in this book to trace their family history. You are a part of their family now, after all. If you have reason to believe that your birth parents are Irish American, and you hope to be able to research that side of your heritage, be sensitive when approaching your adoptive parents for information. Assure them that your goal is only to find out more about your heritage, not to seek out a new family. They may have some information about your birth parents, but it is probably very limited. To obtain more substantive information about your birth parents, you will have to take the legal step of unsealing your adoption records, which in most states cannot be done until you are eighteen years old. As an adult, you will also be able to sign up on an adoption register, if you choose to do so, and you will be matched up with your birth parents if they have also signed up. Above all, be patient and sensitive to the feelings of the family that has raised you.

Resources

STARTING YOUR EXPLORATION

Breffney, Brian, general ed. *Ireland: A Cultural Encyclopedia*. **New York: Facts on File, 1983.**

A useful, quick reference guide to things Irish and cultural. Some entries are very brief, while others give a fuller story.

Cavan, Seamus. *The Irish-American Experience.* **Brookfield, CT: Millbrook Press, 1993.**

Full-color illustrations and personal narratives help to tell the story of Irish Americans.

Conlon-McKenna, Marita. *Under the Hawthorne Tree.* **New York: Holiday House, 1990.**

During the time of the Great Famine, three children are left alone when their mother goes to find their father, who is working on the roads. Dispossessed and sent to the workhouse, the children escape and begin a long journey to find two great-aunts.

Donlon, Pat, et al. *The Lucky Bag: Classic Irish Children's Stories.* **Dublin: The O'Brien Press (US distributor-Dufour Editions), 1984.**

Twenty stories or excerpts include folktales, fairy tales, and more modern stories of adventure, excitement, and growing up.

Franck, Irene M. *The Irish-American Heritage.* **New York: Facts on File, 1989.**

Firsthand accounts and period illustrations detail the

history of Irish Americans, describing their immigration, settlement, and contributions to American culture.

Quinn, Bridie, and Cashman, Seamus, eds. *The Wolfhound Book of Irish Poems for Young People*. **Dublin: Wolfhound Press (Dufour Editions), 1990.**

A great selection of poems. Includes a subject index.

Riehecky, Janet. *Irish Americans*. **New York: Marshall Cavendish, 1995.**

Why did the Irish come to America? What were their lives like in their new land? The author discusses these issues as well as family values, religious traditions, and accomplishments of Irish Americans.

Ross, Anne. *Druids, Gods and Heroes from Celtic Mythology*. **New York: Peter Bedrick Books, 1994.**

A collection of forty-three Celtic myths, legends, and folktales, including the ancient tales of Ireland.

Watts, J. F. *The Irish Americans*. **New York: Chelsea House, 1995.**

Senator Daniel Patrick Moynihan, himself an accomplished Irish American, wrote the introduction to this well-illustrated overview of the Irish immigrant experience.

ADOPTION

Adoptees and Birthparents in Search
P.O. Box 5551
West Columbia, SC 29171
803-796-4508

Adoptees' Liberty Movement Association (ALMA)
P.O. Box 154 Washington Bridge Station
New York, NY 10033
212-581-1568

Adoptees' Search Right Association
Xenia, OH 45383
419-855-8439

Adoptees Together
Route 1, Box 30-B5
Climax, NC 27233

Adoption Cycle
401 East 74th Street
New York, NY 10021
212-988-0110

Adoptive Families of America
3333 Highway 100 North
Minneapolis, MN 55422
24-hour hotline: 800-372-3300

American Adoption Congress
1000 Connecticut Avenue NW
Washington, DC 20036

Askin, Jayne, with Molly Davis. *Search: A Handbook for Adoptees and Birthparents*, 2d ed. Phoenix, AZ: Oryx Press, 1992.

> The authors provide advice to adoptees seeking their birth parents, and address family issues, laws, and overcoming obstacles.

Cohen, Shari. *Coping with Being Adopted.* New York: Rosen Publishing Group, 1988.

> Explores questions most frequently asked by children and young adults who have been adopted, such as: How do I locate my birth parents? Should I attempt to contact them? How will they react when they see me again? Also discusses how to cope with feelings of frustration, abandonment, and the lack of a stable identity experienced by many children who have been adopted. Features a section of personal interviews with young adult adoptees.

Concerned United Birth Parents
200 Walker Street
Des Moines, IA 50317

International Soundex Reunion Registry
P.O. Box 2312
Carson City, NV 89702

National Adoption Information Clearinghouse
11426 Rockville Pike, Suite 410
Rockville, MD 20852

People Searching News
J. E. Carlson and Associates
P.O. Box 22611
Fort Lauderdale, FL 33335
305-370-7100

A bimonthly newsletter for adoptees, birth parents, and others seeking biological relatives.

Chapter 2
Your Irish Immigrant Ancestors

Family history is more than just names and dates. We are trying to place our ancestors in a place and a time. To learn more about why they left, how they travelled, and why they felt the way they did about certain issues, we need to learn about the place they left behind.

The good family historian or genealogist starts by learning more about the country of his or her origin. In the case of your ancestors, this is Ireland. This chapter contains a very brief version of Irish history and the conditions that the immigrants found when they arrived in the United States. The **Resources** list other materials that you may want to read as background information.

The Geography of Ireland

Ireland's history is linked to its geography. This second-largest island in the British Isles is surrounded by the Atlantic Ocean, St. George's Channel, and the Irish Sea. The only political boundary on the island is the border between Northern Ireland and the Republic. The Republic of Ireland is an independent nation and is a member of the United Nations and the European Union. Northern Ireland is part of Great Britain.

The island can be compared to a saucer because it has a mountainous coastline which slopes down to lush green valleys. The climate is moderate, with the Gulf Stream keeping the temperatures in July and August at approximately sixty-five degrees, while in January and February it averages forty degrees. The "forty shades of green" that the visitor sees are a result of frequent rainfall. Mild temperatures and plentiful rainfall are the farmer's delight. Agricul-

St. Patrick is the patron saint of Ireland. Legend has it that he banished all snakes from Ireland, but science has proved that the lack of snakes in Ireland is simply a result of its geography.

ture in Ireland produces cattle, hogs, sheep, poultry, turnips, sugar beets, and, of course, potatoes, to name just a few of the crops. Recently, Ireland has become a center for printing and the assembly of electronic devices. These new industries need skilled labor and provide an alternative to emigration as a means to find work. The tourist trade is one of the major industries in Ireland, with large numbers of foreign visitors coming each year. Some of them, like you, are searching for their heritage.

Early History

The first people who came to Ireland probably came in approximately 6000 BC and crossed over the narrow channel between Scotland and Northern Ireland. These people were hunters and fishermen living near the rivers and lakes. They hunted the giant elk and other animals that roamed the grasslands and, later, the dense forests. In approximately 3500 BC a new group came to Ireland. These New Stone Age people arrived with skills such as domesticating animals, farming, making pottery, and tanning hides. They lived in wooden houses, and built large stone tombs, such as Newgrange, for their dead.

By 1800 BC, more people were coming to Ireland. Metal workers discovered rich deposits of copper and tin in the regions that are now the counties of Cork and Kerry. These substances were important during the beginning of the Bronze Age. Trading with England's Cornwall and the coast of Northern Spain began, and Irish goods started to circulate in Europe.

In approximately 700 BC, the Celts invaded Ireland. They had moved into the British Isles from their original territory in Central Europe. The Celts were a fierce group who imposed their will on the inhabitants of Ireland. The iron weapons they brought were adapted to make ards. The ard was a rough type of plow that made farming easier. Large areas could be planted with less work. Celtic society was based on the language that is today called Gaelic. During this period, the Roman Empire conquered the Mediterranean region and invaded France (Gaul) and, later, Britain. Ireland was never invaded by the Romans. The invasion of Britain and the task of subduing the warrior bands living there was costly and time-consuming. Rome had conquered so much territory that the Empire became difficult to govern. It fell into a decline, and no expedition to Ireland was ever launched in the 400 years of the Roman occupation of Britain.

Celtic Society

What was Celtic society like? Celtic Ireland was a patchwork of small kingdoms led by a king, called a ri, and his nobles. This system was typical of many farming societies. These kings would unite to fend off an invader or other enemy. The high king, called the ard-ri, was a later development. He was responsible for settling disputes and calling an assembly of the kings of the smaller kingdoms.

In Celtic society, three groups developed to help the king rule. The Brehons were a group of professional lawyers who settled arguments and decided the law with a complicated system of guarantees and contracts. They maintained a lawful society without a police force. The Filidh, or the poet/bards, held a high position in Celtic society because they kept the oral tradition alive with the history, genealogy, and stories of the people. The Druids were the early priests of Ireland. They held both fire and water as sacred elements. The Druids were the teachers of the pre-Christian era.

The Early Church

St. Patrick is the patron saint of Ireland, but there is much to be discovered about his life and times. Patrick was born the son of a Roman Briton in approximately 400 AD. He was captured by Irish raiders and made a slave when he was about sixteen. According to legend, he tended sheep in County Antrim for six years before he escaped back to Britain. While he was a slave, Patrick turned to prayer for his consolation, and upon gaining his freedom, he decided to

This rock structure in County Kerry is one of hundreds built in Ireland during the Middle Ages. Called cloghans, the stone huts were used by monks for meditation and the payment of penance. Many of the huts still stand today and are popular tourist attractions.

become a priest. In his *Confession*, he wrote that he had dreams or visions which compelled him to return to Ireland. While the date of his return and his missionary work are not documented, it is generally accepted that he traveled throughout Ireland from 432 to 461 AD.

St. Patrick brought Christianity to Ireland, and it was the development of many monasteries and abbeys that helped maintain and preserve knowledge during the period known as the Dark Ages, or Early Middle Ages (c. 450–750 AD). Abbeys are monasteries under the supervision of an abbot or convents (societies of nuns) under the supervision of an abbess. The monasteries started out as a small collection of people and buildings. The men were priests, monks, and novices (young men in training). Monks are a special male group in the Roman Catholic Church whose members take vows of poverty, chastity, and obedience. They are considered co-owners of the monastery's community property. Irish monasteries became centers of learning and attracted men from all over Europe. Some of the most famous were Glendalough, Kells, Clonmacnois, and Cong.

Life in a monastery or abbey was very harsh and austere. The location of many of the monasteries was often an isolated place where worldly influences would not intrude or tempt these holy men. The monks were required to live very simply and to pray often. A monastery consisted of a church, refectory, cells (living quarters), school, and a library. The living conditions were rustic.

As time went on, the European monastic orders came to Ireland with more traditional Roman practices. They began to build more monasteries. These orders also brought with them copies of manuscripts for the new libraries. Ireland became a storehouse of knowledge during the Early Middle Ages. While some of the monks worked in the fields to raise food for the community, others worked at copying manuscripts. This was how the *Book of Kells* and the *Book of Durrow* were created. These illuminated manuscripts are copies of the Gospels with hand-drawn, often whimsical illustrations.

The Vikings

Beginning in the late eighth century, the Vikings began to raid the coastal areas of Ireland. They sought the artistic and literary treasures of the monasteries, but they also sought to exploit trading opportunities on the coast of Ireland. The Vikings established a settlement at the mouth of the Liffey River, where Dublin is today. Other formerly Viking towns include Limerick, Waterford, Wicklow, Wexford, and Cork. The contributions of the Vikings include the establishment of a money economy, increased trade with Europe, and the development of towns. Their influence lasted until 1014 AD, when Brian Boru defeated them at Clontarf and created a united Ireland.

The town of Kells, in County Meath, is the site of an ancient monastery founded by St. Columba, whose house is shown above. *The Book of Kells*, a beautifully illuminated manuscript, contains notes on local history and was found in the monastery. *The Book of Kells* is now displayed at Trinity College in Dublin.

The Middle Ages in Ireland

With the defeat of the Vikings in 1014, Ireland began to revert to its previous state as a country ruled by many kings. The country was flourishing economically but not politically. No strong leader emerged who could control all the different factions that existed. When Brian Boru was killed in 1014, his sons were not able to command the loyalty and the power that would have allowed them to rule effectively.

In 1166, the king of Leinster, Dermot MacMurrough, fled to England to look for allies who would help him regain the throne of Ireland, which he had lost in a complicated feud. The Irishman wanted to be king but the only way he could achieve this was to get a Norman from England to help him. He located Strongbow, Richard FitzGilbert de Clare, who was the Earl of Pembroke. Dermot and Strongbow struck a bargain. Dermot would become king of Ireland, and in return Strongbow would marry Dermot's daughter, Aoife, and would succeed Dermot as king. Dermot died in 1171 and Strongbow inherited his title.

The Normans

The Normans were Scandinavian Vikings who conquered the northwest region of France, today known as Normandy, in the mid-ninth century. The pagan Normans adopted Christianity as well as the language and social customs of France before turning northward to invade England in 1066. In the Battle of Hastings, William, Duke of Normandy, defeated the Anglo-Saxon king Harold II and assumed the English crown as William I. The period following William's invasion is known as the Norman Conquest of England.

Once the English throne was usurped by William I, the Norman aristocracy supplanted the English aristocracy. William granted English lands to his Norman barons, thereby securing their loyalty and fulfilling the need for social cohesion among the relatively small group of Norman conquerors. The Normans are believed to have introduced the medieval social system known as feudalism to England, whereby land was granted by a feudal lord to a vassal (a feudal tenant) in exchange for military services or other obligations. Feudalism established a relationship of mutual protection, obligation, and loyalty between social groups. The Normans made significant contributions to the cultural development of England, particularly in the fields of architecture, language, and literature. A vast number of stone castles, abbeys, and churches were constructed during the Norman reign in a style that was heavily influenced by Romanesque architecture. Norman French was adopted as the language of the English court, aristocracy, and polite society. It also became the language of Anglo-Norman literature and influenced the development of the English language.

In 1171, Henry II of England invaded Ireland, thus initiating the Anglo-Irish struggle that has continued through to modern times.

The Norman Empire lasted until 1204, when England once again became a separate kingdom. Norman rule left behind a legacy of greater political stability, unprecedented economic prosperity, and cultural enrichment.

Ireland and the English

The Anglo-Norman conquest of Ireland took approximately ten years. The Anglo-Norman conquerors brought with them the feudal system, under which all land belonged to the king, who could grant ownership to whomever he wished. Each landlord could divide his land into smaller holdings and give them to his loyal nobles. These men could then divide the land into even smaller shares. This created a tenant/landlord relationship that would have a powerful impact on Ireland in the nineteenth century.

The introduction of feudalism brought the castle into Ireland. These fortified structures, complete with moats, were where feudal landlords presided. Scattered over the Irish countryside, many are in ruins, but some have been converted into homes and inns. The Anglo-Normans also brought a central government, with a parliament and administrative system. The Viking settlements had grown with the influx of trade, and what had been small villages could then truly be called towns.

From the 1300s to the 1500s, a series of small battles continued. The Irish never accepted the rule of the English crown. There were sporadic outbreaks and rebellions, but they were put down, with harsh consequences for the rebels. As a result of a rebellion in 1534, Henry VIII made all the landowners of Ireland surrender their lands, which he would grant back to them when they pledged their loyalty to him. They would have to accept his Protestant (Anglican) church and renounce Roman Catholicism to keep their lands. The landowners became Protestant in order to keep their lands, while the tenants remained Roman Catholic.

Roman Catholicism was briefly restored in England in 1555 shortly after Mary I ascended the throne. Mary I, who had always remained loyal to the Roman Catholic faith, aroused violent opposition among her political and religious opponents when she repealed Henry VIII's laws establishing Protestantism in England. She became known as "Bloody Mary" as a result of her persecution of Protestants. Nearly 300 Protestants were burned at the stake during her reign.

Religious tensions were intensified when the tide turned toward Protestantism once again during the reign of Elizabeth I. Elizabeth I required that the Irish Parliament acknowledge her as the "Head of the Church of Ireland" (which was Protestant). More rebellions broke out during these bloody times in Ireland, as the English government gradually extended its effective control of the island outward from Dublin.

The Plantations

What is a plantation? To most Americans the word brings to mind the large beautiful houses and land worked by slaves in the southern United States. To the Irish, it refers to a large tract of land, which was settled by strangers. The Ulster Plantation began with the "Articles of Plantation" in 1609. After many rebellions, skirmishes, and European wars, the English government decided to reward their soldiers by giving them land in Ireland. The settlers were English and Scottish people who brought their customs of farming and their Protestant faith to the area. Since these settlers had been soldiers, there was a defense force readily available. The problem was that King James I gave to the settlers land that he had taken from Catholic landowners who would not change their religion. Thus the seeds of the "Troubles" were planted.

The settlers built towns with walls to protect themselves. They became active in the political process in Ireland and soon controlled the Irish government at the local and national levels. The Irish were not pleased. In 1641, a rebellion of the Irish Catholic residents against the English and Protestant settlers was put down. It brought Oliver Cromwell and the victorious parliamentary army to Ireland in 1649 after the execution of King Charles I. Cromwell and his English soldiers came to avenge the massacres of the Protestant settlers. In the nine months that Cromwell stayed, the countryside was destroyed and the people were terrorized and dispossessed of their lands. The Irish Parliament was abolished, and other repressive laws were enacted.

The Restoration

After Cromwell died in 1658, the Catholic Church in Ireland began to reorganize. Charles II became king, and when he died, his brother James II succeeded him. James II was Catholic. The rights of Catholics were still limited, but James began to make changes. He allowed Catholics to live in the towns again, but they could not hold political office. James was unpopular because of his religion, and anti-Catholic hysteria forced him to flee to France. William of Orange and his wife, Mary, James's daughter, became king and queen of England. However, James was not finished. In 1689 he arrived in Ireland from France and marched to Londonderry in Northern Ireland. When his army met King William's men at the Boyne River on July 12, 1690, James was soundly defeated. The Battle of the Boyne was a turning point in Irish history, as it solidified the political control of the Protestants in Ireland.

The Penal Laws kept many Irish Catholics in the position of tenant farmers, who could be evicted for not paying rent to their landlords. This engraving depicts Irish peasants seizing an evicted tenant farmer's potato crop in County Kerry.

Penal Times

In 1691, the first of the Penal Laws was passed. These laws made it extremely difficult for Roman Catholics to own land. A Catholic could not inherit land if there was any Protestant heir. Leases were restricted to thirty-one years. Catholics could not enter the armed forces or a number of other professions. Other restrictions dictated that they could not teach school, have their children educated either in Ireland or abroad, or own guns.

Later, in 1697, all Catholic bishops were banished, and parish priests had to register with the government in order to continue their work. Mass rocks and hedge row schools, often referred to in tales handed down over the generations, come from this chapter of Irish history. Mass rocks were places in the countryside where Catholics gathered for Mass when the Penal Laws made it difficult for them to congregate in church. Hedge row schools were small country schools, often held outdoors in the summer, where priests taught Catholic children who were not allowed to attend ordinary schools.

The Penal Laws, which were intended to rid Ireland of the Catholic Church, did just the opposite. They strengthened Catholics' loyalty to their church and hardened their resistance to Protestant domination. The laws were still in effect until the Catholic Emancipation led by Daniel O'Connell in 1829. The Catholic Emancipation freed Catholics from the oppressive regulations that restricted their participation in many spheres, such as education, politics, and the military.

Prelude to the Great Famine

From 1690 until the Great Famine in 1845, Ireland was still an agriculture-based country. In 1800, Ireland was made part of Great Britain by the "Acts of Union." There was no longer an Irish parliament—only a British one. Many of the Irish parliamentary representatives were Protestant landowners.

The Irish population was growing, but the economy was in decline. Landholdings of the tenant farmers were being divided and subdivided. In many cases, the land on which the house sat and the small garden next to it were all the tenant farm family could call their own. Tenant farmers grew wheat, barley, and other crops, but these were used to pay rent and taxes. The potato with a little milk and butter was the centerpiece of most Irish meals.

The Great Hunger

The Great Famine, or the Great Hunger, started in September 1845 in Wexford and Waterford. It was caused by a blight that ruined the potato crop, and it spread rapidly. There had been smaller famines in 1843 and 1844, but this one lasted until 1849, and the effects were still being felt when the American Civil War began in 1861. The blight caused the potato in the field to turn black and die almost instantly. Unlike previous fungal infections, the blight also destroyed the harvested potatoes. The population of Ireland

This engraving illustrates the plight of the Irish during the Great Famine and their plea for help from the United States.

was approximately 8 million people in 1845 when the blight struck. By 1851 almost 4 million had died or left Ireland. If the lack of food did not kill a person, famine-related diseases such as typhus and cholera did. Relief efforts by the government were almost non-existent and added to the distrust of government by the people. The many absentee landlords of the large estates lived in England and left their estates to be cared for by managers or agents. Some of these absentee landlords were interested only in the income from their property, which supported their lifestyles in England. The gap between the landlords and their tenants began to widen even further. Not all landlords fell into this category, however. Many did what they could for the people living on their estates.

The period from 1851 to 1922 saw significant change in Ireland. The famine had broken down many institutions and opened the way for new ideas. In 1867, the Fenians, one of the secret societies in support of Irish independence, staged an uprising. Many of its military leaders were former soldiers in the American Civil War. The uprising was a failure, mainly because of lack of weapons and funds.

Politically, the situation in Ireland had begun to change. The Irish National Land League, which was working to prevent sudden rent increases and evictions, sought to make the tenants owners of their land. The Home Rule League gained support in Ireland for the cause of Irish independence. However, the British government imprisoned the leaders of these movements. There was a constant struggle for power. The secret societies waited for just the right moment.

The Easter Rebellion in 1916 was one of these moments. On Easter Monday, a small group of men captured the General Post Office in an effort to disrupt communications. A few other government buildings were captured as well. A proclamation was read, which declared Ireland a republic. The rising was unsuccessful, but it did inspire many. The Irish Republican Army (IRA) came into existence shortly after the Easter Rebellion. This nationalist organization was

Spectators in Dublin examine the ruins of the General Post Office in the aftermath of the 1916 Easter Rebellion. The Rebellion failed, and was followed by guerrilla warfare and harsh reprisals by British troops, but it did succeed in mobilizing the independence movement and its leaders.

formed by Michael Collins, who organized the rebels involved in the Easter Rebellion into a new unit that was to become the military arm of the Sinn Féin party. From its beginning, the driving force and primary goal of the IRA has been to achieve a united and wholly independent Ireland.

In 1917, a home rule framework was established. With the Anglo-Irish Treaty in 1921, Ireland was divided into the Irish Free State and Northern Ireland. The Irish Free State refused to recognize the partition, however, and by 1922, the conflict led Ireland to a civil war. While it lasted less than one year, it was bloody and harsh. After the civil war, Ireland began to rebuild slowly. The economy faced a postwar slump, and emigration still took many of the best and brightest to other places. From 1922 to 1937, the Irish Free

State existed as a dominion (a self-governing territory) within the British empire. In 1937, a new constitution was ratified which terminated Great Britain's sovereignty in Ireland. In 1948, the Republic of Ireland Act ended Catholic Ireland's membership in the British empire. The Republic of Ireland was formally declared on Easter Monday, 1949. Since then, many of the same problems between the two parts of Ireland have continued. A lack of opportunities and slow economic growth are still part of life in Ireland. But the Irish spirit has not been destroyed by centuries of struggle. Out of Ireland's tumultuous history have emerged some of the world's greatest writers, poets, and achievers in many fields.

Ireland Today

Ireland today is part of the European Union. In 1990, Mary Robinson was elected President of the Republic of Ireland. For decades, the IRA has vehemently opposed the status of Northern Ireland as a separate state under the dominion of Britain through numerous acts of terrorism. There is an active campaign for peace which began with a ceasefire in 1994. The world hopes that the "Troubles" will be resolved in a peaceful manner.

The Irish in America

When did the Irish start coming to America? They were probably at the founding of Jamestown in 1607, or they arrived soon after. Many of the early Irish settlers were merchants or the younger sons of landowners. These men came for land, money, and freedom. George Washington and Thomas Jefferson both had Irish ancestors. American statesman Patrick Henry, who is famous for saying "Give me liberty or give me death," was the son of a well-educated Scots Presbyterian minister who came to the United States from Northern Ireland in protest of the Penal Laws. Pennsylvania founder William Penn granted land to whole groups of Irish people because he hoped that they would serve as a buffer between the Native Americans and the Quakers.

Countess Constance Markievicz, who was married to a Polish count, was one of many Irish women who joined their country's fight for independence from Britain. A member of Sinn Féin, Countess Markievicz was sentenced to death for her role in the Easter Rebellion in 1916 but was released in 1917.

By 1775 there were approximately a quarter of a million Irish people living in America, most of whom were Protestant. There were some Catholic families, but they tended to live in Maryland and Pennsylvania because those colonies granted religious freedom. Language and economic factors were two main reasons why there were so few Irish Catholics in America. Most Irish Catholics were tenant farmers, and their resources were limited. There was also a language barrier; Gaelic was the language of the farm and of the poor. As life in Ireland changed, however, English became the predominant language. As a result, more Irish Catholics immigrated to the United States because they now spoke the language and found it easier to assimilate.

After the American Revolutionary War, the United States became a haven for leaders like Wolfe Tone and others who were working to free Ireland. But the average Irish person was primarily interested in earning a living and becoming an American citizen. He or she was not worried about conditions in Ireland unless they affected the family left behind.

The Uprising of 1798, an unsuccessful rebellion led by Wolfe Tone, affected the United States in many ways. Because they had supported the rebellion, some wealthy Irish families and many artisans and craftsmen immigrated to the United States or Canada. The Irish in the United States then found a rallying point and became a political force. New York's *Truth Teller* and Boston's *Pilot* were two newspapers that voiced the concerns of an Irish electorate.

Many Irish came to American cities and found that they lacked the skills needed to be employed in the factories. Many worked as day laborers and lived in deplorable conditions. Jobs such as street cleaning, unloading cargo, construction, and other dangerous occupations went to Irish immigrants. As the Irish immigrants adapted to their new country, they became more American than many Americans. They filed their petitions for citizenship as soon as they were able. Most Irish men became citizens, creating a large voting bloc.

Irish children cheer the establishment of home rule for Ireland in 1921 while waving American flags, underscoring the role of Irish American individuals and associations in helping southern Ireland achieve its freedom.

The Great Famine in Ireland in 1845 had a chilling effect on the American Irish. The newspapers carried stories of what was happening, but the full impact was not felt until 1846. In that year, hundreds of weak and emaciated people began to arrive in American port cities. Ships that carried large numbers of people infected with cholera or typhus were turned away. These "coffin ships," as they were called, would sail to Canada and drop their passengers off there. The healthy immigrants would work odd jobs to pay for food or lodging. Friends and family who had immigrated earlier were eager to help. The Irish had a very close-knit community, and the new immigrants were quickly integrated into American society.

Prior to 1850, all Irish people were called Irish. But with the rising number of poor, illiterate Catholic Irish immigrants, the term "Scots" or "Scotch Irish" began to be used by the Protestant Irish to distinguish themselves from the

Catholics. The Scotch Irish were the descendants of Scottish immigrants to Ireland in the seventeenth century. The Irish who arrived in the United States earlier did not want to be identified with the later waves of immigrants.

While there were some organizations that could assist the new arrivals, most were not founded until the mid-1850s. The Catholic Church was also unable to give immediate help. Before this influx of Catholics, there were only a few churches, some small schools, and very limited church-sponsored services. This would later change under Archbishop John Hughes. The Archbishop was born in Ireland and was self-educated. He saw the need for Catholic schools and churches to help the new immigrants.

While the Church provided one kind of help, the Young Irelanders, the Fenian Brotherhood, and other radical groups that formed during this period provided another. Lecture tours, meetings, and newspapers told the average Irish American citizen about conditions in Ireland. They were reminded of the troubling events back in Ireland. Although there were various plans to free Ireland from British rule, the main concerns were to raise a citizen army and to provide military training.

In 1861, the American Civil War provided many Irish Americans with opportunities to change their lives. Soldiers and sailors earned steady incomes, had opportunities to advance, and, in the later years of the war, received bonuses for enlisting. Enlistment was the fastest way to become a citizen, and that was the greatest incentive. The Irish Brigade and the Fighting 69th distinguished themselves in the Battle of Fredericksburg and other important battles. Many units were composed of Irish immigrants and Irish Americans. There was discrimination against the Irish in the military, and as a result, the Irish units were often given the worst duty. But those who survived were able to use their new skills to improve their lives.

After the Civil War, the Irish continued to come to the United States. In many cases they faced the same discrimination as earlier immigrants had, but now there was help. The earlier immigrants shared what they had learned with

The Reverend John Carroll, a first-generation Irish American, fought for religious freedom for Catholics in the United States in the nineteenth century. Few Irish Americans in the early part of the century were Catholic; most were Protestant.

the newcomers. County societies were formed in the 1870s. These societies became places for people from Galway or Sligo or Waterford to meet. These societies also put the new immigrants in touch with citizens who knew of places to live and available jobs.

During the 1870s and 1880s many labor unions were formed, and Irish immigrants became some of the earliest members. Irish Americans were now moving into skilled positions in the factories as well as in civil services such as fire and police departments. As they gained an economic foothold, the Irish began to build more schools for their children. Education became a major factor in the ever-improving lives of the Irish immigrants and Irish Americans. While religious discrimination continued, the development of the Catholic school system provided Irish immigrants with the tools they needed to succeed.

In the late 1800s, emigration from Ireland slowed but did not end. New waves of immigrants from southern Europe now bore the brunt of discrimination, while the English-speaking Irish were more accepted. The struggle with England was still a reality for many Irish. The cause for freedom was burning in the hearts of many. These people supplied some of the monies and arms used finally to free the predominantly Catholic southern Ireland. The United States also produced Eamon de Valera, the first President of the Republic of Ireland and one of the leaders of the Easter Rebellion. De Valera was born in New York of an Irish mother and a Spanish father. After the Easter Rebellion in 1916 and the civil war, the Irish continued to emigrate. The stagnant economy and lack of jobs in Ireland forced many to leave.

Today, some 37 million people in the United States claim Irish heritage. Their contributions can be found all around you, from music and dance to theater to industry.

Irish Women Immigrants

Ireland has long been a large source of women emigrants. Beginning in the 1840s and continuing today, Irish women have emigrated on their own, and have found work to support themselves and pay passage for other single women relatives and friends. There is no other country whose women have set up such a network for immigration and resettlement.

At the forefront of this system was Vere Foster. During the second half of the nineteenth century, she started a special fund to sponsor women immigrating to the United States. She and her followers were responsible for the relocation of some 23,000 Irish women.

The final years of the famine brought changes to Ireland that affected women negatively. When small land holdings were consolidated into larger ones, children could no longer hope to inherit pieces of their parents' land. Only the eldest son had any hope of getting a plot of his own. As a result, a woman could not expect to marry and be supported by her husband. In fact, women often supported their fathers and brothers, working as domestic servants and in textile factories. Domestic work was particularly coveted because it included a place to stay and allowed female workers more personal freedom than they would have had living at home with their families. These domestic abilities were the skills Irish women would later use when they came to the United States.

And come they did. By 1900, the number of female Irish immigrants landing in the United States was greater than the number of male Irish immigrants.

The 1920s were a period of particular conservatism toward women in Ireland. Although independence was won from Britain, women were not freed from their socially accepted roles. Many had participated in the revolution, but they did not win their own liberty. They were destined to a life of working the family plot with their bare hands for no pay, or, if they were fortunate, finding wage work in cities. Irish cities suffered particular poverty in the 1920s, so there was little hope of work in the urban areas.

The Catholic Church reinforced the subservient position of women. With little opportunity to marry, many women remained single and in the service of their extended family. All of the land they worked and the products they made were owned by men.

This is not to say that a woman could not aspire to great achievements without leaving Ireland in the first decades of the twentieth century. Hanna Sheehy-Skeffington and Countess Constance Markievicz were important leaders in the

Large numbers of single Irish women, destined to a fate of toiling as domestic workers or for their families if they stayed in Ireland, sought better lives in the United States. These four Irish women disembarked in Boston in 1921.

Sinn Féin movement for Irish independence. In 1923, six Northern Irish women were elected to the British Parliament.

For most, however, it was a difficult life. Northern Ireland, too, was a tough place for women in the first half of the twentieth century. Most worked in textile mills sixty hours per week, then had to cook, clean, and care for their families. Jobs were so scarce that when a woman had a baby, she had to be back at the factory within two days or she would lose her job. Many women could not afford to buy the sheets and tablecloths they made at the mill. The United States was an attractive alternative to many young women.

World War II gave Irish women a taste of freedom, because their country needed their skills and energy while the men were at battle. Many women joined nursing units or other non-combat positions and got a chance to travel and have adventures. After such an experience, many Irish women could not face returning to their conservative, patriarchal society. The 1950s marked another wave of Irish women immigrants to the United States.

The most recent wave of Irish women immigrants began in the 1980s and can be attributed to the feminist movement that has affected all of the Western world. As they have for generations, single Irish women today find work in the United States as nannies and housekeepers. The difference is that today they come with high school and even college educations, and save their salaries to pay for graduate school or other professional training programs in the United States.

Irish American women have made many important contributions to American society. Irish American women writers include Kate Chopin, Louise Imogen Guiney, Phyllis McGinley, Mary McCarthy, and Flannery O'Connor. Just a few of the many famous Irish American women of stage and screen are Helen Hayes, Irene Dunne, Mia Farrow, Susan Sarandon, Ava Gardner, Anjelica Huston, Maureen Stapleton, Patricia Neal, Tatum O'Neal, Grace Kelly, Maureen O'Hara, and Brooke Shields. In other fields, we find presidential lobbyist Susan Brophy; community organizer Mary Brosnahan; children's advocate Sister Kay Crumlish; Adele Dalsimer, head of the Department of Irish Studies at Boston College; columnists Maureen Dowd and Mary McGrory; publisher Nan Talese; and U.S. ambassador to Ireland, Jean Kennedy Smith.

Prominent Irish Americans

The Irish have made important contributions to American society since their earliest days in the United States.

There were not many Irish in America during the colonial period, and few of those were Catholic. John Carroll (1737–1832) was a courageous exception. Carroll was born and raised in Maryland and believed he had a calling to the Catholic clergy. In that colony, however, organized Catholic churches and Catholic high schools and colleges were illegal.

Carroll was determined and went to Flanders (today Belgium) to learn to be a priest. He then returned to America and travelled around the colonies, seeking out Catholic families and helping them to practice their faith. Eventually he was made an archbishop. Carroll was also important in assisting his close friend Benjamin Franklin in plans for the American Revolution. After independence was won, he founded Georgetown University.

J. Augustin Daly (1838–1899) was a respected Irish American entrepreneur during a period when Irish people were, in general, not well respected or trusted in the United States. In the second half of the nineteenth century Daly was a theatrical manager, known mostly for his company's productions of Shakespeare on Broadway. There was even a theater named after him. During that same period, Irish American Mathew Brady pioneered the use of the camera. If you have ever seen a photograph from the Civil War or of President Abraham Lincoln, chances are it was taken by Brady or one of his students.

At the turn of the century Robert Joseph Flaherty, born in Michigan, began explorations of subarctic eastern Canada. Besides his physical adventures and geographical research, Flaherty contributed to the art of filmmaking. In 1922 he made the first feature-length documentary film, called *Nanook of the North.*

Irish Americans have made enormous contributions to twentieth-century arts and letters. Georgia O'Keeffe, born in Wisconsin, is one of the most important American painters. Her college training in abstract design can be seen in her work, which features images from the American Southwest.

Eugene O'Neill received many awards throughout his distinguished career as a playwright. He was a three-time Pulitzer Prize winner and was honored with the Nobel Prize for Literature in 1936.

Although her career was cut short by an early death, Flannery O'Connor left us two novels and two brilliant collections of short stories. O'Connor's fiction tends toward brutal satire, drawing from her experience growing up

New York-born Eamon de Valera served as president of Ireland from 1959 to 1973 after working actively to achieve independence for Ireland as the leader of Sinn Féin. He was greeted by Irish Americans in South Carolina during a 1920 visit.

Roman Catholic in the American South during the 1930s and 1940s.

Other Irish American writers who have delighted readers for generations include F. Scott Fitzgerald, Finley Peter Dunne, John O'Hara, Mary McCarthy, Jack Higgins, and Mary Gordon. And American cinema would not be what it is today if we did not have the talents of Bing Crosby, Gene Kelly, Spencer Tracy, Pat O'Brien, Ryan O'Neal, Aidan Quinn, John Cusack, Robert Redford, Jack Nicholson, and many other Irish American actors.

On the cutting edge of medical science, Charles Horace Mayo and William James Mayo were surgeons at the turn of the twentieth century. Besides their excellent work in medicine, these brothers left a legacy that is still celebrated worldwide: the Mayo Clinic in Minneapolis and the University of Minnesota's Mayo Foundation for Medical Education and Research.

Perhaps Irish America's most obvious contribution to American society is in the field of politics. Eamon de Valera, the major Irish political figure of the twentieth century, was

American-born. Justice Sandra Day O'Connor joined the U.S. Supreme Court in 1981. When she was appointed, she became the first woman to hold the position. Daniel Patrick Moynihan was born in Oklahoma in 1927, and was raised in New York City. He has compiled an impressive record as a Democratic official. Most notably, he served in the Department of Labor under Presidents John F. Kennedy and Lyndon B. Johnson, and joined the U.S. Senate in 1976.

John F. Kennedy and his family make up a stellar collection of Irish Americans involved in politics. JFK won a Pulitzer Prize for *Profiles in Courage,* his book on politicians who have defied popular opinion and voted according to their consciences. When he became the thirty-fifth President of the United States, he was the youngest man and the first Roman Catholic ever to hold that post. He was assassinated in 1963. His brother Robert was U.S. Attorney General from 1961 to 1964, and made a bid for the presidency but was assassinated on the campaign trail. Edward (Ted) Kennedy, another brother of JFK, has also served in the U.S. Senate. JFK was not the only U.S. President of Irish descent; sharing that distinction have been Andrew Jackson, James Polk, James Buchanan, Chester Arthur, William McKinley, Woodrow Wilson, Richard Nixon, Ronald Reagan, and Bill Clinton.

This is only a small sampling of Irish American men and women who have made a difference in the United States. These immigrants and children of immigrants have left their mark on every walk of life. Their spirit, their industry, even their language and sense of humor, have affected the development of American society in profound ways.

Resources

IRISH HISTORY

Ardagh, John. *Ireland and the Irish*. New York: Penguin, 1995.

A sweeping survey of forty years of profound change in the Irish Republic, including the changing role of women, the fight for the Irish language, and the reconciliation movement in the North.

Beckett, J. C. *The Making of Modern Ireland: 1603–1923*. London: Faber and Faber, 1981.

The focus of this work begins with the death of Elizabeth I in 1603 and continues up to the end of the civil war in 1923. This is a good overview of Irish history. The bibliographical essay contains numerous additional sources of information.

Bottigheimer, Karl S. *Ireland and the Irish: A Short History*. New York: Columbia University Press, 1982.

The broad sweep of Irish history is presented in a very readable overview. The reader will gain a better understanding of the problems facing Ireland in the late twentieth century.

Cahill, Thomas. *How the Irish Saved Civilization*. New York: Doubleday, 1996.

This book reminds us about the Irish monks who spent their days copying manuscripts and preserving the knowledge of the ancients. This is a witty look back at medieval life and culture and its impact on modern society.

De Paor, Liam. *The Peoples of Ireland: From Prehistory to Modern Times.* **Notre Dame, IN: University of Notre Dame Press, 1986.**

This is a concise history of the people who make up the Irish nation. This work touches on the major events and developments in Ireland's past. The author discusses the social, cultural, and religious life of Ireland. He uses his background in archaeology to explain the significance of the prehistoric and medieval periods of Irish history.

Fitzgibbon, Constantine. *Red Hand: The Ulster Colony.* **London: Joseph, 1971.**

A general survey of the history of the six counties that constitute Ulster.

Foster, R. F. *Modern Ireland, 1600–1972.* **London: Penguin Press, 1988.**

This scholarly work on Irish history was on the best-seller list in Ireland for a year. Foster combined his own research with that of recent scholars to create a new interpretation of Irish history. His effective literary style makes the discussion of the social, political, religious, and economic aspects of Irish life very readable.

———, ed. *The Oxford Illustrated History of Ireland.* **New York: Oxford University Press, 1992.**

This is a richly illustrated account of Irish history. It has a good bibliography for further research.

Harbison, Peter. *Pre-Christian Ireland: From the First Settlers to the Early Celts.* **New York: Thames and Hudson, 1988.**

The history of the earliest people in Ireland may be obscured by the lack of written documentation, but these people did leave archaeological evidence. This work surveys the evidence as well as describes current research and excavations.

Kee, Robert. *The Laurel and the Ivy: The Story of Charles Stewart Parnell and Irish Nationalism.* **London: Hamish Hamilton, 1993.**

Charles Stewart Parnell was a Protestant landowner who became a prominent member of Parliament. He supported the home rule proposals and land reform, and was a major voice for Ireland. This biography discusses both his political and personal life.

Llewelyn, Morgan, and Scott, Michael. *Ireland: A Graphic History.* **Rockport, MA: Element, 1995.**

This history of Ireland is illustrated in a cartoonish style. It highlights the significant events in Irish history and links them to the present. From the opening chapter, which describes a bomb blast that injures two people, to the final page, with an illustration of the 1994 cease-fire, this readable book blends history and culture into a unique account that makes history come alive.

MacManus, Seamus. *The Story of the Irish Race.* **New York: Devin-Adair, 1921. Reprinted, 1979.**

This book was written in 1921 "in an attempt to sketch a rough and ready picture of the more prominent peaks that rise in Ireland's past . . . ", according to the foreword. The author uses each chapter to illustrate a specific place, event, or person in Irish history. It is well documented and indexed. The author provides an intelligent, sympathetic view of Irish history.

Moody, T. W., and Martin, F. X., eds. *The Course of Irish History*, **rev. ed. Niwot, CO: Roberts Rinehart, 1994.**

This is an illustrated overview of Irish history, beginning with the earliest people and leading the reader to the present-day problems and events.

O'Connor, John. *The Workhouses of Ireland: The Fate of Ireland's Poor.* **Dublin: Anvil Books, distributed by Irish Books and Media, 1995.**

The workhouse was a feared and hated institution in Ireland. It was supposed to assist the poor by providing work. This book explains how workhouses were established, how the funds were raised to pay for them, and why the people hated them with such passion.

Ranelagh, John. *Ireland: An Illustrated History.* **New York: Oxford University Press, 1981.**

A very readable and well-illustrated history of Ireland.

Sharkey, Olive. *Old Days, Old Ways: An Illustrated Folk History of Ireland.* **Dublin: O'Brien Press, 1985.**

The folklore of a country reflects the struggles and hopes of its people. This is a nostalgic look back at a bygone era in Ireland.

Young, Arthur. *A Tour in Ireland 1776–1779.* **Shannon, Ireland: Irish University Press, 1970.**

This is a facsimile edition taken from the 1892 fourth edition of this book. Young recorded his observations as he traveled about the countryside. He presents descriptions of the agricultural and social conditions in Ireland in the late eighteenth century. Young writes in the style of his day and the text can be tedious at times.

THE GREAT HUNGER

Campbell, Stephen J. *The Great Irish Famine.* **Strokestown Park, Ireland: The Famine Museum, 1994.**

The Famine Museum of Strokestown produced this booklet to educate its visitors about the Great Famine. The preceding social conditions, the blight itself, the ensuing famine, and its impact on the nation are examined here. It is well illustrated with period engravings.

Gallagher, Thomas. *Paddy's Lament.* **New York: Harcourt Brace Jovanovich, 1982.**

If you want to learn about the human side of the Great Famine, this book should be on your list. It is a very readable account of how the famine occurred and what life was like when the immigrants arrived in New York. The author presents a balanced account while showing the reader the ethnic and religious discrimination that the Irish faced.

Kinealy, Christine. *This Great Calamity: The Irish Famine, 1846–1852.* **Dublin: Gill & Macmillan, 1994.**

This is a fresh look at the famine. Kinealy takes a long look at the darker side of the British government's response. Her report is very readable and thought-provoking.

Poirteir, Cathal, ed. *The Great Irish Famine.* **Dublin: Mercier Press, 1995.**

The impact of the famine is examined from many different perspectives, including politics, medicine, folk memory and traditions, and literature.

Scally, Robert. *The End of Hidden Ireland: Rebellion, Famine, and Emigration.* **New York: Oxford University Press, 1995.**

The town of Ballykilcline in County Roscommon is the focus of this book, which examines the impact of the Great Famine on a small rural community. Life prior to and during the famine are described. The eviction of tenants and their resistance is documented. After their homes were destroyed, many of the people were forced to immigrate to New York. Scally has done painstaking research and has written a readable account of life in rural Ireland.

Somerville, Alexander. *Letters from Ireland During the Famine of 1847.* **Edited by K. D. M. Snell. Dublin: Irish Academic Press, 1994.**

Using personal accounts of the famine, Somerville captures the pathos of the rural poor. First published in 1852, this book provided a chilling look at the hardships of the poor and was an attempt to understand the cause of so much suffering. The reader will begin to understand why Ireland suffered so dearly.

MODERN IRISH HISTORY AND THE TROUBLES

Adams, Gerry. *Free Ireland: Towards a Lasting Peace*, rev. ed. Dingle, County Kerry: Brandon, 1995.

Gerry Adams, president of Sinn Féin, lays out his views of how to end the violence in Ireland.

Barry, Tom. *Guerrilla Days in Ireland: A Personal Account of the Anglo-Irish War*. Boulder, CO: Roberts Rinehart, 1995.

In 1921, the "Flying Columns" of the Irish Republican Army were volunteers fighting a larger and better equipped British Army. This account of the West Cork Flying Column was written by its commander. He describes the hit-and-run tactics used to increase the pressure on the government to withdraw the British troops in the southern twenty-six counties.

Bell, J. Bowyer. *The Irish Troubles: A Generation of Violence: 1967–1992*. New York: St. Martin's Press, 1993.

A massive, monumental history of the Troubles, based on interviews, research, and observation. This is a history filled with drama and disaster. A good source if you want both an overview and a lot of detail on the issue.

———. *The Secret Army: The IRA, 1916–1979*, rev. ed. Dublin: Academy Press, 1979.

The standard work on the history of the IRA.

Carlton, Charles, ed. *Bigotry and Blood: Documents on the Ulster Troubles.* **Chicago: Nelson-Hall, 1977.**

A collection of political tracts, manifestoes, and various government declarations dating from the seventeenth century to 1977.

Caufield, Max. *The Easter Rebellion: Dublin 1916,* 2d **ed. Boulder, CO: Roberts Rinehart, 1995.**

On Easter Monday morning of 1916, a column of men marched down Dublin's O'Connell Street toward the General Post Office. There, these citizens took a stand for their independence. This is a detailed account of that dramatic moment in Irish history. The reader can explore the how and why of this event.

Conroy, John. *Belfast Diary: War as a Way of Life.* **Boston: Beacon Press, 1995.**

In this very readable and personal account, a journalist offers a street-level view of the war in Northern Ireland, looking at how ordinary people are affected.

Coogan, Tim Pat. *Eamon de Valera: Long Fellow, Long Shadow.* **London: Hutchinson, 1993.**

Biography of the man who forged the independence movement and became the first president of the Republic of Ireland.

————. *The IRA: A History.* **Boulder, CO: Roberts Rinehart, 1994.**

A thorough reference on the history of the IRA.

————. *The Man Who Made Ireland: The Life and Death of Michael Collins.* **Boulder, CO: Roberts Rinehart, 1992.**

A biography of a central figure in modern Irish history, Michael Collins, who forged independence for the Republic of Ireland.

Dewar, Michael. *The British Army in Northern Ireland*. **London: Arms and Armour Press, 1985.**

Lt. Colonel Dewar, who served in Ulster, discusses the tactics, weapons, and strategy of the British Army in Northern Ireland.

Farrell, Michael. *Northern Ireland: The Orange State*, **2d ed. London: Pluto Press, 1980.**

A classic history of Northern Ireland from its inception to the 1970s.

Kee, Robert. *The Green Flag: A History of Irish Nationalism*. **London: Weidenfeld and Nicholson, 1972.**

Modern Irish political histories tend to be biased, but this one has gained the respect of both Republican and Unionist scholars. The bibliography, which is arranged by historical time period, is a good source for further reading.

Keogh, Dermot. *Twentieth-Century Ireland: Nation and State*. **Dublin: Gill and Macmillan, 1994.**

A detailed survey of Irish politics and a social history of the state, with an emphasis on the Republic.

Lee, J. J. *Ireland 1912–1985: Politics and Society*. **New York: Cambridge University Press, 1989.**

An award-winning, massive study of Irish society (North and South) in the twentieth century. It discusses Irish politics in the context of economic, social, and intellectual history.

McCafferty, Nell. *Peggy Deery: An Irish Family at War*. **Pittsburgh: Cleis Press, 1988.**

Peggy Deery, the mother of thirteen children, was a Catholic woman living in Derry, Northern Ireland. This personal and powerful account of her life traces the story of the Troubles and the way people, especially women, have withstood the wars waged around them.

McCann, Eamonn. *War and an Irish Town*, **rev. ed. Boulder, CO: Pluto Press, 1993.**

This classic account of growing up Catholic in a Northern Irish ghetto paints a vivid picture of the early days of the civil rights movement in Northern Ireland, as peaceful protest developed into armed insurrection.

Miller, David, W. *Church, State and Nation in Ireland 1898–1921.* **Dublin: Gill and Macmillan, 1973.**

The Catholic Church's role in Irish politics during the years prior to independence is examined in this work. The importance of the Catholic Church in late twentieth-century Ireland can be traced back to this time period.

Morrison, Danny. *West Belfast: A Novel.* **Boulder, CO: Roberts Rinehart, 1995.**

Set in the streets of war-torn Belfast in 1969, this novel powerfully portrays working-class home life in Belfast during the Troubles.

O'Brien, Brendan. *The Long War: The IRA and Sinn Féin, 1985 to Today.* **Syracuse, NY: Syracuse University Press, 1995.**

An up-to-date history of the events in the ongoing conflict, including recent peace talks.

O'Connor, Fionnuala. *In Search of a State: Catholics in Northern Ireland.* **Belfast: The Blackstaff Press, 1993.**

Written by a journalist born and still living in Northern Ireland, this readable book focuses on the lives of Catholics in the province. Based on interviews with fifty Catholics living in Belfast and elsewhere, it gives a genuine sense of the lives of ordinary people.

Shannon, Michael Owen. *Northern Ireland.* **World Bibliographical Series, Vol. 129. Santa Barbara, CA: Clio Press, 1991.**

An annotated bibliography of Northern Ireland with more than 1,900 entries. Topics range from prehistory, religion, politics, and the Troubles, to the arts and major personalities.

Younger, Calton. *Ireland's Civil War*. London: Fontana Press, 1979.

Ireland won her freedom with the Anglo-Irish Treaty in 1921. Unfortunately, a civil war broke out in 1922 as the different factions sought power. The war lasted a little more than one year. The new constitution, approved in December, 1922, defined the relationship between England and Ireland. This work explores the causes and the implications of the war and its legacy in Ireland today.

SPECIAL TOPICS IN IRISH HISTORY

Beale, Jenny. *Women in Ireland: Voices of Change*. Bloomington: Indiana University Press, 1987.

A portrayal of the changing experience of Irish women, told through in-depth interviews with twenty-seven women from fourteen to eighty-seven years old. The women talk about their lives and the differences between the generations.

Brown, Richard Howard. *I Am of Ireland*. Niwot, CO: Roberts Rinehart, 1995.

An autobiographical account of one man's trip to Ireland in search of a connection with the country and its people. His family had come from Ireland three generations earlier.

Coulter, Maureen, and Hoff, Joan, eds. "Irish Women's Voices: Past and Present." *Journal of Women's History*, Vol. 6, No. 4, Vol. 7, No. 1, Winter/ Spring 1995.

This collection of scholarly articles focuses on individual Irish women and trends in their changing roles. These strong articles reflect the voices of women from medieval Ireland to the present.

Curtis, Liz. *The Causes of Ireland: From the United Irishmen to Partition.* **Belfast: Beyond the Pale Publications, 1994.**

A new radical history of the Irish struggle for independence. All the major conflicts and campaigns are explained and enlivened with stories of people, both famous and unknown.

De Paor, Liam. *Portrait of Ireland: Ireland—Past and Present.* **New York: St. Martin's Press, 1985.**

A roving look at the country through the eyes of the author. He discusses prehistory, myths, Dublin, the provinces, literature, and other topics.

Joyce, P. W. *English as We Speak It in Ireland,* **2d ed. Dublin: Wolfhound Press, 1988.**

An excellent book for a real flavor of Ireland. Originally published in 1910, it has a colorful dictionary of sayings, an anthology of proverbs, tidbits from folklore, and unique Hiberno-Englishisms.

Kelly, A. A. *Wandering Women: Two Centuries of Travel Out of Ireland.* **Dublin: Wolfhound Press, 1995.**

Women have travelled out of Ireland and returned to tell their tales since the 1790s. The thirty-seven adventurous women profiled in this book include Anna Jane Thornton, who posed as a male sailor to get to New York, and Daisy Bates, who studied the lives of Australian aborigines.

MacMahon, Bryan, trans. *Peig: The Autobiography of Peig Sayers of the Great Blasket Island.* **Dublin: The Talbot Press, 1973.**

Peig, a traditional storyteller, was born in a remote coastal town. She married a fisherman from Blasket Island and lived there for forty years. A moving story of life in a harsh environment, this is a classic text which children in Ireland read in Gaelic.

Mollan, Charles; Davis, William; and Finucane, Brendan, eds. *Some People and Places in Irish Science and Technology.* **Dublin: Royal Irish Academy, 1985.**

A dictionary of brief biographies of Irish scientists who have made important contributions to their field.

———. *More People and Places in Irish Science and Technology.* **Dublin: Royal Irish Academy, 1990.**

Additional Irish scientists and their contributions.

Verdon, Michael. *Old Cork Remembered: Shawlies, Echo Boys, the Marsh and the Lanes.* **Dublin: O'Brien Press; Dufour Editions, 1994.**

A look back at one of Ireland's major cities in its heyday. Illustrated with photos dating to the turn of the twentieth century.

Younger, Calton. *A State of Disunion.* **London: Frederick Muller, Ltd., 1972.**

The life stories of four important leaders of modern Ireland: Arthur Griffith, founder of Sinn Féin; Michael Collins, who led the armed fight for independence; James Craig, who led the fight of Protestants; and Eamon de Valera, who fused the independence movement and became president.

THE IRISH IN AMERICAN MILITARY HISTORY

Beaudot, William J. K., and Herdegen, Lance J. *An Irishman in the Iron Brigade.* **New York: Fordham University Press, 1993.**

James Patrick Sullivan volunteered for the war in 1861 and served for four years in the Iron Brigade of the West.

After he returned home to Wisconsin, he wrote recollections of his war experiences, which are presented here. In addition, there is historical and biographical information that puts his experience into perspective.

Bilby, Joseph G. *Remember Fontenoy!: The 69th New York and The Irish Brigade in the Civil War.* Hightstown, NJ: Longstreet House, 1995.

If you are interested in the American Civil War, this is a fun book, and it is one of the few books to tell the story of this famous brigade. Includes dozens of portraits and a bibliography on the topic.

Jones, Paul. *The Irish Brigade.* New York: Robert B. Luce, 1969.

The Irish Brigade played a memorable role in the American Civil War. This is a historic account of their activities.

Miller, Robert Ryal. *Shamrock and Sword: The Saint Patrick's Battalion in the U.S.-Mexican War.* Norman: University of Oklahoma Press, 1989.

An intriguing story of American soldiers who decided to fight in the Mexican Army—many of them immigrant Irishmen. The American government treated them all as deserters to be punished, while the Mexican government saw them as heroes and erected a monument to them.

Welsh, Peter. *Irish Green and Union Blue: The Civil War Letters of Peter Welsh.* Edited by Lawrence F. Kohl and M. C. Richards. New York: Fordham University Press, 1986.

A member of the Irish Brigade during the American Civil War, Peter Welsh wrote many letters to his family. Through these personal letters, the reader gets a vivid picture of both the war and the person.

IRISH IMMIGRATION AND IMMIGRANTS

Barnes, John A. *Irish-American Landmarks: A Traveller's Guide.* **Detroit: Visible Ink Press, 1995.**

A wonderfully fun book to guide your travels around the United States in search of Irish American connections, or to read through for fascinating tidbits of Irish-Americana. For example, did you know that the first woman in the United States memorialized with a statue was the Irish-born Margaret Gaffney Haughey, who helped New Orleans orphans, or that the Choctaw Nation Museum has exhibits on the types of assistance the Choctaws sent to the Irish during the Great Famine?

Birmingham, Stephen. *Real Lace: America's Irish Rich.* **New York: Harper and Row, 1973.**

This is a tale of the making of wealthy Irish families in America. Includes some family photos.

Bradley, Ann Kathleen. *History of the Irish in America.* **Secaucus, NJ: Chartwell Books, Inc., 1986.**

The Irish in America as seen through the achievements of Irish Americans, illustrated with plenty of photographs. Includes famous people from Henry Ford to Ronald Reagan.

Clark, Dennis. *Hibernia America: The Irish and Regional Cultures.* **Westport, CT: Greenwood Press, 1986.**

Irish immigrants moved all over the United States, adapting to where they lived and contributing to local life. This is a good overview of Irish American life in all regions of the country.

———. *The Irish in Philadelphia.* **Philadelphia: Temple University Press, 1973.**

This classic work examines ten generations of Irish Americans in Philadelphia. Clark was one of the first to chronicle the Irish with a regional focus.

————. *The Irish Relations: Trials of an Immigrant Tradition.* **East Brunswick, NJ: Associated University Presses, 1982.**

A portrayal of the price paid by Irish workers for the development of the industries, businesses, and urban institutions in Philadelphia, and those workers' efforts to maintain their own dignity and ties to their heritage. Provides insight into the toll paid for progress, how active subcultures can affect a city, and how ethnic traditions are maintained in an urban community.

Cooper, Brian E., ed. *The Irish-American Almanac and Green Pages*, rev. ed. New York: Harper and Row, 1990.

The almanac section is a compendium of facts and lists: festivals, 100 notable Irish Americans, Irish food, Gaelic names, landmarks, and more. The Green Pages include more than 1,200 sources nationwide for Irish-related goods and services.

Dolan, Jay P. *The Immigrant Church: New York's Irish and German Catholics, 1815–1865.* Baltimore: Johns Hopkins University Press, 1975.

In 1865, nearly one-half of New York City's population was Irish and German Catholics. The Church played an important role in immigrants' lives. This work examines the role of religion in strengthening group life in these communities, the development of the Church in the city, and the relationship between urban growth and church growth.

Doyle, David Noel, and Edwards, Owen Dudley, eds. *America and Ireland, 1776–1976: The American Identity and the Irish Connection.* Westport, CT: Greenwood Press, 1980.

A good collection of essays on the relationship between the United States and the Irish, with topics ranging from the Fenian Brotherhood, the relationship between the Irish and the Church, to Irish Americans in business, the military, the theater, and other fields.

Dunne, Finley Peter. *Mr. Dooley and the Chicago Irish*. Edited by Charles Fanning. Washington, DC: The Catholic University of America Press, 1987.

The journalist Finley Peter Dunne first created the character of Martin Dooley in a newspaper in 1893. These stories of Mr. Dooley described the life and customs of the late nineteenth century, and were full of character sketches of Irish immigrants of the time. These sketches are written in everyday language—a kind of brogue—that makes them a bit difficult to read, but reading them aloud provides a flavor of the era.

Elias, Stephen. *Alexander T. Stewart: The Forgotten Merchant Prince*. Westport, CT: Praeger, 1992.

A biography of the Irish-born founder of the first department store.

Emmons, David M. *The Butte Irish: Class and Ethnicity in an American Mining Town, 1875–1925*. Urbana: University of Illinois Press, 1989.

The story of Butte, Montana's large and assertive Irish immigrant population, showing how they ran the town, the miner's union, and the largest of the mining companies.

Fallows, Marjorie R. *Irish Americans: Identity and Assimilation*. Englewood Cliffs, NJ: Prentice-Hall, 1979.

An examination of the issue of ethnic identity and how Irish Americans have adapted to the American context.

Fitzpatrick, D. *Irish Emigration 1801–1921*. Dublin: Economic and Social History Society of Ireland, 1984.

Emigration was one of the great formative factors in modern Irish history: at least 8 million people left between 1801 and 1921. This scholarly assessment synthesizes specialized studies to address this issue.

Fitzgerald, Margaret E., and King, Joseph A. *The Uncounted Irish: In Canada and the United States.* **Toronto: P. D. Meany, 1990.**

Challenging much of accepted Irish American scholarship, the authors claim that the Irish settled in the rural United States and Canada earlier, in greater numbers, and at a higher economic level than most historians acknowledge. Twenty well-researched essays.

Gordon, Michael A. *The Orange Riots: Irish Political Violence in New York City, 1870 and 1871.* **Ithaca, NY: Cornell University Press, 1993.**

On July 12th in 1870 and 1871, groups of Irish Protestants and Catholics clashed when Protestants marched to commemorate victory in 1690 at the Battle of the Boyne. The battle had confirmed Protestant ascendancy in Ireland. Discussing the causes and consequences of these bloody Orange Riots, this book captures the texture of Irish New York after the American Civil War.

Griffin, William D. *The Book of Irish Americans.* **New York: Times Books, 1990.**

What have the Irish brought to America? Here is a fun book about the contributions of famous and not-so-famous Irish Americans. Who developed the first American department store? What were the names of the Irish American soldiers who fought against the United States in the U.S.-Mexican War of 1847? Griffin provides lists of Irish Americans who have distinguished themselves in sports, politics, business, and other fields. His discussion of Irish names, heraldry, and the role of Irish Americans in the U.S. military will be of particular interest to genealogists.

————, ed. *The Irish in America 550-1972.* **Dobbs Ferry, NY: Oceana Publications, Inc., 1973.**

A very concise chronology of major historical facts in the development of the Irish American community. This outline is enhanced by statistical and documentary material in the second part of the book. These documents give a real flavor to the issues raised, through pieces from newspapers, journals, and public speeches.

————. *A Portrait of the Irish in America.* **New York: Charles Scribner's Sons, 1981.**

A very readable overview of Irish life in the United States. Photographs, cartoons, and drawings are accompanied by a concise text.

Handlin, Oscar. *Boston's Immigrants: A Study in Acculturation.* **New York: Atheneum Publishers, 1968.**

A classic case study of the first Irish ghetto in the United States. South Boston continues to be a residential stronghold of Irish Americans. Many recent immigrants from Ireland have settled there.

Hoobler, Dorothy, and Hoobler, Thomas. *The Irish American Family Album.* **New York: Oxford University Press, 1995.**

Like a family album or scrapbook, this book tells the story of the "old country," new life in the United States, and Irish contributions to the United States. Through period photos highlighting family accomplishments, both the famous and not so famous are portrayed.

King, Joseph A. *Ireland to North America: Emigrants from West Cork.* **Lafayette, CA: K and K Publications, 1994.**

Describes a typical early nineteenth-century Irish emigrant family from a remote parish in southwest Cork: their life in Ireland, emigration to Canada, and eventually, to the United States.

Maguire, John F. *The Irish in America*. **New York: Arno Press, 1974.**

Originally published in 1868, this is a valuable source of information on conditions and attitudes of early Irish immigrants.

Malone, Russ. *Hippocrene USA Guide to Irish America*. **New York: Hippocrene Books, 1994.**

A fun guide to take along on trips, with 905 Irish American landmarks related to famous Irish Americans or Irish American heritage. You're bound to find something near you. Includes hours, phone numbers, and brief information on each site.

McCaffrey, Lawrence. *The Irish Diaspora in America*. **Washington, DC: Catholic University of America Press, 1984.**

A useful general history of Irish American society, from a discussion of the causes of emigration to the issues of Irish nationalism and Catholicism.

———. *Textures of Irish America*. **Syracuse, NY: Syracuse University Press, 1992.**

A very readable portrayal of the contributions of the Irish to American society.

———; Skerrett, E.; Funchion, M. F.; and Fanning, C. *The Irish in Chicago*. **Chicago: University of Illinois Press, 1987.**

Examines the history, religion, politics, and literature of one of Chicago's most influential ethnic groups. Irish Americans like mayors Edward J. Kelly, Martin J. Kennelly, Richard J. Daley, and Richard M. Daley have long dominated the city's politics.

Meagher, Timothy J., ed. *From Paddy to Studs: Irish-American Communities in the Turn of the Century Era, 1880–1920*. **Westport, CT: Greenwood Press, 1986.**

After a general introduction to Ireland during the turn of the century, this book contains scholarly articles on Irish living in various places in the United States, such as Lowell, Massachusetts; Chicago; and San Francisco.

————, and Bayor, Ronald, eds. *New York Irish: Essays Toward a History*. Baltimore: Johns Hopkins University Press, 1995.

Essays on the impact of events in the world, the United States, and Ireland on the Irish in New York.

Miller, Kerby A. *Emigrants and Exiles: Ireland and the Irish Exodus to North America*. New York: Oxford University Press, 1985.

A standard reference for those interested in understanding who emigrated, why, and what the results were. In this social history of Irish emigration from the 1600s to the early 1900s, Miller explores the causes of Irish emigration and its impact on the people, on Ireland, and on the United States. Emphasis is on the "ordinary" emigrants; the author has drawn from their personal letters, diaries, songs, and folklore.

————, and Wagner, Paul. *Out of Ireland: The Story of Irish Immigration to America*. Washington, DC: Elliot and Clark, 1994.

A wonderfully colorful book, it uses letters, photographs, and other archival material to describe the experiences of Irish immigrants in Ireland and the United States.

Mitchell, Arthur. *JFK and His Irish Heritage*. Dublin: Moytura Press, 1993.

Traces John F. Kennedy's career and his relationship to Ireland and his Irish heritage. Includes newspaper articles, speeches, and photographs of his visit to Ireland.

Mundy, James H. *Hard Times, Hard Men: Maine and the Irish 1830–1860*. Scarborough, ME: Harp Publications, 1990.

The story of Maine's pre-Civil War Irish immigrants. They came in large numbers from 1832 to the mid-1850s, built railroads, and provided the labor for a period of rapid growth and industrialization. However, they were not welcomed by everyone, prompting anti-Catholic riots and laws.

Niehaus, Earl F. *The Irish in New Orleans 1800–1860*. Baton Rouge: Louisiana State University Press, 1965.

By 1850, 20 percent of the white residents of New Orleans were natives of Ireland. This is an academic account of the socially significant activities of these Irish.

O'Brien, Michael J. *Irish Settlers in America*. 2 vols. Baltimore: Genealogical Publishing Co., 1979.

This is a collection of articles from the *Journal of the American Irish Historical Society*, focusing on seventeenth- and eighteenth-century Irish pioneers. If you had any doubts that the Irish settled in all parts of America in these early years, this should help change your mind. O'Brien uses various records to demonstrate the strong Irish presence: For example, in 1790, residents with a "Mac" surname constituted nearly 20 percent of the population of South Carolina.

O'Donovan, Donal. *Dreamers of Dreams: Portraits of the Irish in America*. Bray, Ireland: Kilbride Books, 1984.

Concise portrayals of twenty-five distinguished Irish Americans in business and academia.

O'Donovan, Jeremiah. *Irish Immigration in the United States: Immigrant Interviews*. New York: Arno Press, 1969.

A reprint of an 1864 book, featuring fascinating interviews with Irish immigrants about their lives in the United States and the parts of Ireland from which they came. Read this book as preparation for conducting your own interviews with relatives (discussed in detail in chapter 5).

Packard, Kathleen Walsh. *Fling Old Glory: The Story of Patrick Walsh, An Irish American Fire Chief.* **Baltimore: Gateway Press, 1992.**

Written by his granddaughter, this is the story of an Irishman who immigrated in 1888 and went on to become Fire Chief and Commissioner under Mayor Fiorello LaGuardia in New York. Gives details of Walsh's personal and professional life; illustrated with family photographs.

Ridge, John T. *Erin's Sons in America: The Ancient Order of Hibernians.* **New York: Ancient Order of Hibernians, 1986.**

The Ancient Order of Hibernians, which existed for nearly 300 years in Ireland, established an American branch in New York in 1836. This is an account of the history of that organization in New York and around the country.

————. *The Flatbush Irish*, **2d ed. New York: Ancient Order of Hibernians, 1990.**

Stories and tales of personalities and experiences of the Irish in the Flatbush section of Brooklyn, New York.

————. *The St. Patrick's Day Parade in New York.* **New York: Ancient Order of Hibernians, 1988.**

A year-by-year description of the St. Patrick's Day parade from 1762 on, with an overview of critical issues surrounding the parade.

Ryan, Dennis P. *Beyond the Ballot Box: A Social History of the Boston Irish, 1845–1917.* **Amherst: University of Massachusetts Press, 1983.**

This book may be of special interest if your ancestors settled in the Boston area. Ryan examines social and political trends among the Boston Irish at a time when the community was booming because of massive immigration.

Wittke, Carl. *The Irish in America.* **New York: Russell and Russell Publishers, 1970.**

A standard reference survey of Irish American history. Rich in detail.

IRISH AMERICAN WOMEN

Camp, Helen C. *Iron in the Soul: Elizabeth Gurley Flynn and the American Left.* **Pullman: Washington State University Press, 1995.**

A biography of America's foremost woman communist. From the early 1900s until her death in the 1960s, Flynn was at the forefront of labor and radical movements. A founding member of the American Civil Liberties Union, Flynn was the only female leader of the Industrial Workers of the World labor union.

Diner, Hasia R. *Erin's Daughters in America: Irish Immigrant Women in the Nineteenth Century.* **Baltimore: Johns Hopkins University Press, 1983.**

Follows women fleeing the Great Famine to settle in the United States. Diner explores post-immigration family life, work and education, the stresses of life, and formal and informal ethnic organizations that helped Irish immigrant women adapt. Diner stresses the elements of Irish cultural tradition that enabled the women to prosper in their new world.

Kraft, Betsy Harvey. *Mother Jones: One Woman's Fight for Labor.* **New York: Clarion Books, 1995.**

Mary Harris, known as Mother Jones, was one of the United States' most dynamic and effective union organizers. Immigrating to the United States in the early 1840s, Mother Jones made public the plight of children working in textile mills, and urged coal miners, steel mill workers, and workers in other industries to fight for their rights. With many photographs, this book tells the story of Mother Jones's struggles.

Nolan, Janet A. *Ourselves Alone: Women's Emigration from Ireland 1885–1920.* **Lexington: University Press of Kentucky, 1989.**

> A very human account of a generation of young women immigrants to the United States, many of whom had a choice between a marginal existence at home or a new life in another world. These young women were often helped by female relatives who had already emigrated.

O'Carroll, Ide. *Models for Movers: Irish Women's Emigration to America.* **Dublin: Attic Press, 1990.**

> One of the few books to focus specifically on Irish women emigrants. The emphasis is on twentieth-century emigrants. Based on interviews with Irish emigrant women, the voices of these women tell powerful stories of the emigration experience.

FICTION AND LITERATURE

Bolger, Dermot, ed. *Ireland in Exile: Irish Writers Abroad.* **Dublin: New Island Books, 1993.**

> A collection of work by Irish writers set in all parts of the world, including Australia, Cambodia, New York, Italy, and Disneyland.

Bradley, Anthony, ed. *Contemporary Irish Poetry*, **2d ed. Berkeley: University of California Press, 1988.**

> This collection focuses on poetry after Yeats.

Casey, Daniel J., and Casey, Linda M., eds. *Stories by Contemporary Irish Women.* **Syracuse, NY: Syracuse University Press, 1990.**

> These stories point to the contradiction between provincial Ireland and Ireland as a modern European state, and the complexities of women's lives in both.

———, and Rhodes, Robert E., eds. *Modern Irish-American Fiction: A Reader.* **Syracuse, NY: Syracuse University Press, 1989.**

Writings from twenty-one Irish Americans, beginning at the turn of the century. A good introduction to the field, with bibliographic information for further reading.

Deane, Seamus, general ed. *The Field Day Anthology of Irish Writing.* **3 vols. Derry: Field Day Publications, 1991. (Distributed by W. W. Norton.)**

The most comprehensive anthology of Irish writing published. Provides an overview of Irish writing from 500 AD to the present.

Fallis, Richard. *The Irish Renaissance.* **Syracuse, NY: Syracuse University Press, 1977.**

From around 1885 to 1940, many Anglo-Irish writers produced important work in many genres. This book gives an overview of the writers of this period, their work, and the literary movement in which they participated.

Fallon, Peter, and Mahon, Derek, eds. *The Penguin Book of Contemporary Irish Poetry.* **New York: Penguin Books, 1990.**

This collection focuses on poetry in Ireland since 1950.

Fanning, Charles, ed. *The Exiles of Erin: Nineteenth-Century Irish-American Fiction.* **Notre Dame, IN: University of Notre Dame Press, 1987.**

A good collection of writing that includes work from three groups: those coming before the famine, the famine generation, and the children of the famine generation.

———. *The Irish Voice in America: Irish-American Fiction from the 1760s to 1980s.* **Lexington: University Press of Kentucky, 1990.**

An overview of the work of Irish American authors and their place in American literature.

Flanagan, Thomas. *The End of the Hunt.* **New York: Warner Books, 1994.**

Using historical and fictional characters, the author gives the reader insight into the events and conflicts that led to the Irish civil war in 1922.

———. *The Tenants of Time*. **New York: Warner Books, 1988.**

How can three men from a small rural community impact a nation? This is the story of three friends who joined the Fenian movement to free Ireland. In 1867 the Fenian Uprising began, but the movement failed and each man's life took a different direction. The rich descriptions of the countryside and the compelling story tell the reader more about the reasons for the uprising than a history text.

———. *The Year of the French*. **New York: Holt, Rinehart, and Winston, 1979.**

The Uprising of 1798 was started by the United Irishmen, who were influenced by Wolfe Tone, a young Protestant lawyer from Dublin. The United Irishmen watched as England and France were at war again. Their hope was that the French would be able to help them defeat the English. This was a very bloody rebellion, but it was also the first time that both Catholics and Protestants united to try to free their homeland.

Forkner, Ben, ed. *Modern Irish Short Stories*. **New York: Penguin Books, 1980.**

A collection of contemporary Irish short stories.

Gantz, Jeffrey, trans. *Early Irish Myths and Sagas*. **New York: Dorset Press, 1981.**

A collection of fables from long ago that survived through oral tradition and were eventually written down. The language sometimes sounds ancient; the stories are a mix of reality and magic.

Glassie, Henry, ed. *Irish Folktales*. **New York: Pantheon Books, 1985.**

Many things can be learned about a people from their folktales. Glassie has selected 125 tales from throughout the island that best express the Irish character.

Harrington, John P., ed. *Modern Irish Drama*. New York: W. W. Norton, 1991.

If you are interested in modern Irish drama, this might be a good place to start. This volume includes reprints of the complete texts of twelve plays by major Irish playwrights, including Yeats, Shaw, and Beckett.

Heany, Marie. *Over Nine Waves: A Book of Irish Legends*. London: Faber & Faber, 1994.

An appealing retelling of traditional Irish tales of violence and romance.

Keane, John B. *Irish Stories for Christmas*. Boulder, CO: Roberts Rinehart, 1994.

In this collection of fifteen original stories, the popular Irish playwright captures the essence of Ireland during the holidays. These are not traditional Christmas tales, but stories about the lives of ordinary Irish country people during the holiday season.

Kennelly, Brendan, ed. *The Penguin Book of Irish Verse*, 2d ed. New York: Penguin Books, 1981.

An anthology of Irish and Anglo-Irish verse from the seventeenth to the twentieth centuries.

Kinsella, Thomas, ed. and trans. *The New Oxford Book of Irish Verse*. New York: Oxford University Press, 1986.

Presents a vast range of Irish poetry from both languages, beginning with pre-Christian poetry in Old Irish and ending in the twentieth century.

Llywelyn, Morgan. *Bard: The Odyssey of the Irish*. New York: Tom Doherty Associates, Inc., 1984.

Reworking ancient myths and legends, this is a magically fictitious tale of the coming of the Irish to Ireland and the men and women who made the island their own.

————. *Grania: She-King of the Irish Seas*. **New York: Ivy Books, 1986.**

Grace O'Malley of Grania, in the Irish tradition, had a passion for the sea. She was a bold pirate who fought the English. In any time period Grania would have been a heroine, but this was the sixteenth century and her greatest enemy was Elizabeth I. This is a fictionalized biography of one of the most daring women in Irish history.

————. *The Lion of Ireland*. **New York: Berkley Books, 1979.**

Brian Boru was the first high king of Ireland. He united the tribes to defeat the Vikings and to take rightful possession of all of Ireland. Boru stands out larger than life in this portrait of Ireland at the end of the tenth century. You will learn about the life and times of this man and of the intrigue that surrounded him.

Monaghan, Patricia, ed. *The Next Parish Over: A Collection of Irish-American Writing*. **Minneapolis: New Rivers Press, 1993.**

A collection of fiction, poetry, and essays by fifty-seven Irish American writers.

Monk, Sean C. *The Road Past Wicklow: Stories of the Irish People*. **Santa Barbara, CA: Fithian Press, 1990.**

Entertaining reminiscences of an Irishman who returns to Ireland from England and the United States in search of his past and his heritage. Portrays an Ireland of decades ago.

Murphy, Maureen O'Rourke, and MacKillop, James. *Irish Literature: A Reader*. **Syracuse, NY: Syracuse University Press, 1987.**

An anthology that begins with the eighth century and proceeds up through the twentieth century. Includes brief biographies and bibliographies of the writers.

O'Mara, Michael, ed. *Tales of Old Ireland.* **Secaucus, NJ: Castle Books, n.d.**

An anthology of short stories about life in Ireland before the modern industrial age.

O'Sullivan, Patrick V. *I Heard the Wild Birds Sing: A Kerry Childhood.* **Dublin: Anvil Books, 1991.**

Part local history, part folklore, part calendar of the rural year, these stories evoke a vanished age in Ireland.

Ormsby, Frank, ed. *A Rage for Order: Poetry of the Northern Ireland Troubles.* **Belfast: Blackstaff Press, 1992.**

An anthology of more than 250 poems from nearly seventy leading poets confronting the passionate intensities of the Northern Ireland Troubles.

Quinn, Peter. *Banished Children of Eve.* **New York: Penguin Books, 1994.**

A novel of Civil War New York. The North is about to impose its first military draft, which in New York City will spark destructive riots. The time period is portrayed through the lives of people of the city, many of whom are Irish immigrants.

Taylor, Alice. *Country Days.* **New York: St. Martin's Press, 1995.**

A collection of stories about memories of life in Ireland, by one of the most popular contemporary Irish writers.

Uris, Leon. *Redemption.* **New York: HarperCollins, 1995.**

The struggle for Irish independence as told through the lives of three great families is presented. The author takes you around the world and back to Dublin as the tale unfolds and Ireland becomes free.

————. *Trinity*. **New York: Doubleday, 1976.**

This epic follows three families from 1885 through the Easter Rebellion in 1916. The author describes the passions and the desires of his characters as they interact with each other and play out their country's struggles on a small scale. There is a sense of history that makes the famine and the Easter Rebellion more than events in a textbook.

Yeats, William Butler. *Fairy Tales of Ireland*. New York: Delacorte Press, 1990.

Collected in the nineteenth century by the Nobel prize-winning poet, these twenty fairy tales retain the flavor of the oral tradition from which they came.

DOCUMENTARY VIDEOS

From Shore to Shore: Irish Traditional Music in New York City, 1993. **Available from Cherry Lane Productions, P.O. Box 366, Truckee, CA 96160.**

Examines the continuity and changes that have occurred in Irish traditional music since the turn of the century. Focuses on New York City, mixing historical photos and film footage with contemporary interviews and performances.

Ireland and Your Irish Ancestry, 1992. **Available from the Heritage Corp., 8 Lower Baggot Street, Dublin 2, Ireland.**

A story of the history of Ireland, the landscape, and music. Includes a "Discover Ireland" section with practical information for visitors, and a "General Guide to Irish Family Names."

Out of Ireland, 1995. **Available from Shanachie Entertainment, 37 East Clinton Street, Newton, NJ 07860.**

A two-hour documentary on the history of Irish immigration to America. (Aired on PBS in June 1995.)

Riverdance on Video, 1994. Available from Rego Irish Records and Tapes, Inc., 64 New Hyde Park Road, Garden City, NY 11530.

An immensely popular performance of traditional Irish dancing.

FILMS

The Informer (1935)

A simple-minded hanger-on betrays an IRA leader to earn a payoff that will help him emigrate. He finds that he can escape neither the wrath of his former comrades nor the pangs of his own conscience.

Beloved Enemy (1936)

Amid the turmoil of the 1921 Irish rebellion, the rebel leader steals the heart of a British officer's fiancee.

The Plough and the Stars (1936)

Screen version of the Sean O'Casey play, but, despite the cast, not a match for the original. In 1916 Dublin, amid the Troubles, a man's marriage is threatened when he is appointed to command the nationalist forces.

Angels with Dirty Faces (1938)

Starring James Cagney, Pat O'Brien, Humphrey Bogart, and Ann Sheridan. Two boyhood friends lose track of each other after getting into trouble with the law. When they meet again as adults, one has become a priest, the other a gangster.

The Fighting 69th (1940)

Starring James Cagney, Pat O'Brien, and George Brent. Serving with the famous Irish American regiment in the muddy trenches of France in World War I, a cocky recruit surprises his buddies with heroism that costs him his life.

Going My Way (1940)

Bing Crosby plays a young priest sent out to serve a tough New York parish under the watchful eye of its stingy rector.

Little Nellie Kelly (1940)

A sentimental saga about the feuds within an Irish American family in New York. Judy Garland plays mother and daughter, dying in the former role but turning up eighteen years later as the daughter. In the latter role, she makes peace between her father and grandfather, who have been estranged. Some stereotypical New York cops give a rousing rendition of "It's a Great Day for the Irish."

The Sullivans (1944)

For all its homespun sentimentalism, this is a true story about five Irish American brothers growing up during the 1930s in a working-class neighborhood of an Iowa city. Despite occasional spats among themselves, they are inclined to stick together when any of them are in trouble. When the bombing of Pearl Harbor jolts the United States into World War II, all five brothers enlist in the Navy. All are assigned to the cruiser *U.S.S. Juneau,* and are drowned when the ship is sunk off Guadalcanal. The Navy subsequently named a destroyer the *U.S.S. The Sullivans* in their honor.

A Tree Grows in Brooklyn (1945)

The trials and troubles of a young girl growing up in an Irish American family, the Nolans, in turn-of-the-twentieth-century Brooklyn. Based on the novel by Betty Smith.

Hungry Hill (1946)

Three generations of an Irish family are trapped in an ongoing feud.

Captain Boycott (1947)

Hard-pressed Irish tenant farmers, squeezed to the limit and threatened with eviction, organize to resist oppressive landlords and their agents.

Odd Man Out (1947)

An award-winning, moving drama about an Irish rebel, wounded in a hold-up, who must choose between those who might help him escape and others who would turn him over to the police.

Fighting Father Dunne (1948)

A priest works to help poor boys amid the squalor and violence of an urban slum.

The Quiet Man (1952)

A former boxer returns from the United States to Ireland in search of a peaceful retirement and a wife. A boisterous comedy full of Irish wit and color.

The Last Hurrah (1958)

As Frank Skeffington, the veteran Irish American political boss of a New England town, Spencer Tracy takes to the campaign trail in a final reelection bid. Humorous touches and a variety of well-acted characters complement Tracy's performance.

Shake Hands with the Devil (1959)

A surgeon in 1921 Dublin leads a double life as a secret leader of the IRA and grows attached to violence for its own sake rather than as a means to an end.

The Night Fighters (1960)

As World War II erupts, the IRA revives its activities in a northern Irish village.

Studs Lonigan (1960)

A young Irish American drifter, dissatisfied and without great prospects, grows up amid the fast-paced, sometimes violent surroundings of 1920s Chicago. Based on the trilogy by James T. Farrell.

The Girl with Green Eyes (1963)

Incisive drama about a relationship between a naive Dublin shopgirl and a worldly writer. Good location scenes strengthen the film.

Young Cassidy (1965)

The early Dublin years of Irish playwright Sean O'Casey, from his days as a laborer to the opening of his play *The Plough and the Stars* at the Abbey Theatre. Provides an evocative picture of the Irish capital at the turn of the twentieth century.

Finian's Rainbow (1968)

A leprechaun attempts to find and bring back a pot of gold taken to the United States by an old Irishman and his daughter.

The Molly Maguires (1970)

A detective infiltrates a secret society, which is dedicated to fighting the oppressive system imposed on Pennsylvania coal miners in the 1870s, and exposes its leaders. Based on a true story; many of the participants were Irish Americans. Stars Sean Connery.

Ryan's Daughter (1970)

In 1916 Ireland, a rural schoolmaster's wife falls in love with a British major and is ostracized for betraying her country.

Barry Lyndon (1975)

Directed by Stanley Kubrick. William Makepeace Thackeray's satirical novel was brought to life in one of the most visually stunning movies ever made, though it has less to commend it dramatically. A roguish Irish peasant rises from obscurity to wealth and position during the period of the Seven Years War between England and France, but ultimately he falls from grace.

Hennessy (1975)

A Northern Irish Catholic whose politics are neutral becomes hardened after his wife and child, innocent onlookers at a street riot, are accidentally killed by British gunfire. Vowing revenge, he sets about a plan to assassinate the Queen of England and members of her government.

Cal (1984)

The librarian-widow of a Protestant policeman and a young IRA activist fall in love amid the violence of contemporary Northern Ireland. The film won praise for its superior acting and its intelligent handling of a controversial subject. For mature audiences.

A Quiet Day in Belfast (1984)

A realistic, tension-filled story set amid the urban war waged between British soldiers and IRA members in the Northern Irish capital. Centered around the colorful everyday drama of a betting parlor, the action moves the opposing sides to a brutal, bloody climax.

James Joyce's Women (1985)

This highly praised film presents dramatic portraits of James Joyce's wife and three of his characters, including Molly Bloom.

No Surrender (1985)

Two groups of old-age pensioners, one Orange (Protestant), the other Green (Catholic), find themselves booked into the same Liverpool night spot to celebrate New Year's Eve. The resulting confrontation is frequently hilarious.

The Dead (1987)

Directed by John Huston (this was his last film); starring his daughter, Anjelica Huston. The screen version of James Joyce's memorable short story *The Dubliners*, set in turn-of-the-twentieth-century Dublin.

A Prayer for the Dying (1987)

Starring Bob Hoskins, Mickey Rourke, and Alan Bates. An IRA hit man has second thoughts about his violent life, only to find that both his fellow nationalists and the police have claims on him. A gripping political drama adapted from the book by Jack Higgins. For mature audiences.

My Left Foot (1989)

Daniel Day Lewis won an Oscar for his performance as Christy Brown, a feisty Irish artist-writer born with cerebral palsy. A moving story based on Brown's autobiography.

The Commitments (1991)

A fun musical tale of an ambitious young Dubliner who takes on the challenge of assembling and managing a band made up of other working-class Dubliners who sing 1960s-style soul music. For mature audiences.

In the Name of the Father (1993)

Intense, fact-based account of a youthful Belfast no-good who is picked up by British police and accused of a terrorist bombing he has no knowledge of. Also charts the persecution his family receives. Daniel Day Lewis gives an intense performance. For mature audiences.

The Secret of Roan Inish (1994)

A gentle, charming tale of a girl who is sent to live with her grandparents on the west coast of Ireland and discovers the myths and magic that have affected her family. Works a magical spell.

The Brothers McMullen (1995)

An entertaining film that was made on a shoestring budget, chronicling the lives of three Irish American brothers and their search for love. For mature audiences.

Circle of Friends (1995)

Set in the 1950s. A spirited and individualistic young woman leaves her Irish village to attend university in Dublin and falls madly in love with a handsome lad. He loves her too, but their relationship is impeded by chance and circumstance. For mature audiences.

Chapter 3
Getting Started

The Most Important Person: You

You have decided to start working on your family history, but how do you get started? Where do you go and what do you do? In genealogy, you go from what you know to what you don't know. In some ways, family research is like doing a term paper for school. You will need to use the library, as well as read and analyze different types of information.

Getting Organized

What equipment do you need to get started? You can begin with a notebook and pens or pencils. When you get ready to interview your relatives, a tape recorder or a video recorder and the appropriate accessories will be needed. File folders will also be helpful. You will need one for each family. Later, you will want one for each person. The folders should be acid-free or of archival quality, which means that the acid in the paper will not destroy your notes and other documents. From a genealogical supplier you should be able to purchase pedigree charts and family group sheets, which will make recording information about each family easier. There are special photograph albums that you can buy, or you can purchase archival plastic sheets and then put the photographs in loose-leaf notebooks for the person or family you are working on.

Special Techniques

In genealogy, there are some special techniques that you should know before you start. Surnames are always listed in capital letters, followed by the first name and any middle names. For example, John Patrick Murphy is MURPHY, John Patrick.

Women are known by their birth or maiden names on pedigree charts or family group sheets. This is true no matter how many times a woman married. Mary O'BRIEN, who married John KELLY, Charles SMITH, and Michael RYAN, will be listed as Mary O'BRIEN. This standard is used in order to connect her to her parents. In text, she is referred to as Mary O'Brien Kelly when John is her husband.

Dates are listed by day, month, and year. While it is handy to list dates as 03/17/96, this could mean 17 March 1896 or 1996. To eliminate confusion, follow the standard format of writing first the date, then the month, then the year. For example: 10 June 1970.

Place names should be fully listed, with town, county, and state. When you start working with overseas locations, you will need to add the country. Some examples:

Downington, Chester County, Pennsylvania
Woodside, Queens County, New York City, New York
Rosdoowaun, County Leitrim, Ireland

Starting at Home

What do you know about yourself and your family? In genealogy, you are the most important person. You are number one on the pedigree chart. So start with yourself. Write down the following information about yourself:

- Where were you born? Who are your parents and grandparents?
- Where were you baptized or christened? Who were your godparents? Were your godparents related to you?
- Where do you live? How many times have you moved?
- Do you have brothers and sisters? What are their names and birth dates?

"Why is this important?" you might ask. The answers to these questions will help you fill out your first family group sheet.

An Example of Home Sources:
The Ryan Family

The hardest part of getting started is to know how to do it. This is probably a new form of research for you. We will be using a fictional family, the Ryans, to illustrate how to start your research.

Our searcher is Mary Ann Ryan, who was born in New York City on 16 June 1982. She was baptized ten days later on 26 June 1982. Her parents are Timothy Patrick Ryan and Kathleen Marie Kelly. Mary has two brothers and one sister. Her godparents are Ann Ryan Sullivan, her father's sister, and Thomas Michael Kelly, her mother's brother.

What have we learned? We know Mary's name, date and place of birth, and the names of her parents, including her mother's maiden name. We also know that she has brothers and sisters and we are starting to pencil in some information on her parents' families. To verify this information we need to get copies of her birth certificate and her baptismal certificate. The baptismal certificate will provide the names of her godparents as well as the name of the church.

As Mary looks at the family group sheet, she can begin to fill in the information on her brothers and sister. The family group sheet on page 77 shows the information on Mary's parents, her brother Daniel, and Mary herself. She knows their birthdays, and her mom can tell her more information about them. Since most parents have their children's birth certificates in a safe place, Mary could ask to see them or have photocopies made. Mary's mom located Mary's baby book and brought out a photo album of pictures of her as a newborn baby and at her christening. The picture album and baby book revealed that she was baptized in St. Patrick's Church on Mott Street in New York City. There were more pictures of her family with many aunts and uncles and both sets of grandparents. Identifying these pictures can give Mary many family names and relationships. The pictures can eventually be used to illustrate a family history.

Now Mary can go back another generation by asking her parents for information about when and where they were born. This is the process of identifying the home sources,

Family Group Sheet - 1

Husband -Timothy Patrick RYAN-2

Born (day month year) 2 September 1952	Place Woodside, Queens, New York
Christened	Place
Died	Place
Buried	Place
Married 16 August 1979	Place Paterson, New Jersey
Husband's father	Daniel John RYAN
Husband's mother	Mary Elizabeth O'BRIEN

Wife - Kathleen Marie KELLY-3

Born (day month year) 24 April 1953	Place Paterson, New Jersey
Christened	Place
Died	Place
Buried	Place
Wife's father	James Thomas KELLY
Wife's mother	Ann Frances SULLIVAN

Children List each child (whether living or dead) in order of birth.

Sex-M Daniel James RYAN-4

Born (day month year) 19 July 1980	Place Paterson, New Jersey
Christened	Place
Died	Place
Spouse	
Married	Place

Sex-F Mary Ann RYAN-1

Born (day month year) 16 June 1982	Place New York, New York
Christened 26 June 1982	Place St. Patrick's, Mott Street, New York, New York
Died	Place
Spouse	
Married	Place

which then can be verified by going to the county court-house, city hall of records, a library, or another outside source. When you first get started, write down everything and make notes as to who gave you the information and when and where. This is part of the process of documentation.

In order to obtain more information on previous generations, Mary interviews her parents. She is looking for the same information that she recorded for herself. Her father, Timothy Patrick Ryan, is the next-to-youngest of three girls and two boys. His father was Daniel John Ryan, born in New York, and his mother was Mary Elizabeth O'Brien, born in Ireland. Kathleen Marie Kelly, Mary's mother, is the oldest of four children—two boys and two girls. Her parents are James Thomas Kelly, born in New Jersey, and Ann Frances Sullivan, also born in New Jersey.

Further interviews with Mary's parents and grandparents will reveal more information. Look at family group sheets 2 and 3 to see the new information Mary obtained and how she recorded it. She has recorded information on each set of grandparents and two of their children. On the pedigree chart on page 81, Mary has recorded the information from family group sheets 1 and 2.

Where To Go Next

Verifying the data obtained from home sources is the next step—but where does one go and how does one do it? The library, the county or city hall of records, and the state archives are all places to look. To prepare yourself, you may prefer to read some books about doing this type of research.

Your local library is a good place to start. In the catalog, check under the subject heading "genealogy" for general materials. Materials you will want to look for include newspapers (for obituaries, weddings, and other information that may be helpful), histories of your town or county, directories of residents and/or businesses, and any other local information. Census records and indexes may be available for your local area; if not, the librarian can help you locate them and

Family Group Sheet - 2

Husband -Daniel John RYAN-7

Born (day month year) 14 July 1924	Place New York, New York
Christened	Place
Died	Place
Buried	Place
Married 2 February 1946	Place St. Patrick's, Mott Street, New York, New York
Husband's father	
Husband's mother	

Wife - Mary Elizabeth O'Brien-8

Born (day month year) 3 September 1928	Place Dublin, Ireland
Christened	Place
Died	Place
Buried	Place
Wife's father	
Wife's mother	

Children List each child (whether living or dead) in order of birth.

Sex-F   Ann Marie RYAN-9

Born (day month year) 12 December 1946	Place New York, New York
Christened	Place
Died	Place
Spouse	
Married	Place

Sex-M   John Michael RYAN-10

Born (day month year) 2 July 1948	Place New York, New York
Christened	Place
Died	Place
Spouse	
Married	Place

Family Group Record - 3

Husband -James Thomas KELLY-13

Born (day month year)	Place
15 March 1927	Paterson, New Jersey
Christened	Place
Died	Place
Buried	Place
Married	Place
16 February 1950	St. Patrick's, Jersey City, New Jersey
Husband's father	
	Daniel John RYAN
Husband's mother	
	Mary Elizabeth O'BRIEN

Wife - Ann Frances SULLIVAN-14

Born (day month year)	Place
4 May 1930	Jersey City, New Jersey
Christened	Place
Died	Place
Buried	Place
Wife's father	
	James Thomas KELLY
Wife's mother	
	Ann Frances SULLIVAN

Children List each child (whether living or dead) in order of birth.

Sex-F   Kathleen Marie KELLY-3

Born (day month year)	Place
24 April 1953	Paterson, New Jersey
Christened	Place
Died	Place
Spouse	
Timothy Patrick RYAN-2	
Married	Place
16 August 1979	Paterson, New Jersey

Sex-M   Michael Francis KELLY-15

Born (day month year)	Place
12 November 1954	Paterson, New Jersey
Christened	Place
Died	Place
Spouse	
Married	Place

Pedigree Chart

Name of Compiler _____

Address _____

City, State _____

Date _____

Person No.1 on this chart is the same person as No._____ on chart No._____.

Chart No._____

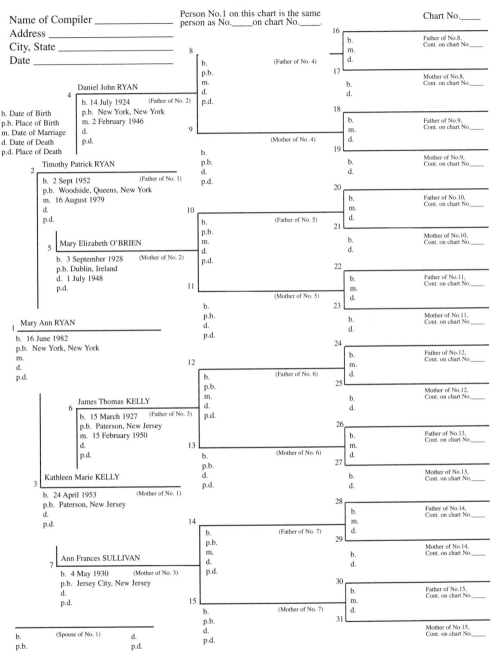

b. Date of Birth
p.b. Place of Birth
m. Date of Marriage
d. Date of Death
p.d. Place of Death

8

Daniel John RYAN

4

b. 14 July 1924   (Father of No. 2)
p.b. New York, New York
m. 2 February 1946
d.
p.d.

2   Timothy Patrick RYAN

b. 2 Sept 1952   (Father of No. 1)
p.b. Woodside, Queens, New York
m. 16 August 1979
d.
p.d.

5   Mary Elizabeth O'BRIEN

b. 3 September 1928   (Mother of No. 2)
p.b. Dublin, Ireland
d. 1 July 1948
p.d.

1   Mary Ann RYAN

b. 16 June 1982
p.b. New York, New York
m.
d.
p.d.

6   James Thomas KELLY

b. 15 March 1927   (Father of No. 3)
p.b. Paterson, New Jersey
m. 15 February 1950
d.
p.d.

3   Kathleen Marie KELLY

b. 24 April 1953   (Mother of No. 1)
p.b. Paterson, New Jersey
d.
p.d.

7   Ann Frances SULLIVAN

b. 4 May 1930   (Mother of No. 3)
p.b. Jersey City, New Jersey
d.
p.d.

b.   (Spouse of No. 1)   d.
p.b.   p.d.

8
b.
p.b.
m.
d.
p.d.   (Father of No. 4)

9
b.
p.b.
d.
p.d.   (Mother of No. 4)

10
b.
p.b.
m.
d.
p.d.   (Father of No. 5)

11
b.
p.b.
d.
p.d.   (Mother of No. 5)

12
b.
p.b.
m.
d.
p.d.   (Father of No. 6)

13
b.
p.b.
d.
p.d.   (Mother of No. 6)

14
b.
p.b.
m.
d.
p.d.   (Father of No. 7)

15
b.
p.b.
d.
p.d.   (Mother of No. 7)

16
b.
m.
d.   Father of No.8, Cont. on chart No._____

17
b.
d.   Mother of No.8, Cont. on chart No._____

18
b.
m.
d.   Father of No.9, Cont. on chart No._____

19
b.
d.   Mother of No.9, Cont. on chart No._____

20
b.
m.
d.   Father of No.10, Cont. on chart No._____

21
b.
d.   Mother of No.10, Cont. on chart No._____

22
b.
m.
d.   Father of No.11, Cont. on chart No._____

23
b.
d.   Mother of No.11, Cont. on chart No._____

24
b.
m.
d.   Father of No.12, Cont. on chart No._____

25
b.
d.   Mother of No.12, Cont. on chart No._____

26
b.
m.
d.   Father of No.13, Cont. on chart No._____

27
b.
d.   Mother of No.13, Cont. on chart No._____

28
b.
m.
d.   Father of No.14, Cont. on chart No._____

29
b.
d.   Mother of No.14, Cont. on chart No._____

30
b.
m.
d.   Father of No.15, Cont. on chart No._____

31
b.
d.   Mother of No.15, Cont. on chart No._____

borrow them using interlibrary loan procedures. Many of the books and other materials listed in the **Resources** sections of this book may be found at your public library or obtained through interlibrary loan.

To get vital records, including birth, death, and marriage records, you will have to go to either the Board of Health, the Hall of Records, or the State Archives. Where you go will depend on the time period for which you need records. The federal government has a leaflet called "Where to Write for Birth, Death and Marriage Certificates." It is available from the U.S. Government Printing Office.

Census records can be helpful, but you must be able to locate your family in 1920 or earlier. Censuses conducted after 1920 are not available to the public to protect the privacy of persons still living. The census was started in 1790 and is taken in years ending with 0. The original purpose of the census was to count the number of people living in an area in order to determine the number of representatives the area should have in the U.S. Congress. The 1920 Federal Census is the most recent federal census available to the public. The older the census records, the less information they contain.

Census records are an accounting of everyone living in a household at a specific time. They can be very helpful to the family historian. The head of the household is listed with his age, occupation, marital status, place of birth, and other information. Data were also recorded about his wife and children. Also listed are any others living with the family, including other relatives, in-laws, servants, and boarders. The census can be a gold mine of information, especially in the days when elderly relatives would live with younger family members. Census records are located at the National Archives or one of its branches. They can also be found in some libraries. Ask your librarian about the availability of census records.

Many of the federal census records have been or are in the process of being indexed. The 1900 and 1920 censuses have a complete Soundex for all names. The Soundex system is a method of indexing names using the first letter of the last name and a code for the next three consonants. This system is explained in greater depth in the census publications. You will need to remember that the 1910 census has a Soundex for all states that did not have vital records and that the 1880 census only has a Soundex for families with children up to ten years of age.

State census records were often done in the years ending with 5, or, if a territory wanted to become a state, a special census might have been done. These census records can be very helpful as you track the family between the federal census records. Unfortunately, most of these records are not indexed. This is why addresses for your family from city directories can help you narrow down the exact address, which will make searching these records easier.

Your local library can also supply you with materials on the history of your town or county. If an uncle was the mayor or a noted businessman, there may be something written about him. These clues can help you when you are at an impasse with your direct ancestral line.

The Hall of Records

Depending on where you live, the Hall of Records may be called the Clerk of Court, the County Clerk's Office, or a variety of other names. This is where local documents about governmental happenings are gathered. Deeds, petitions for naturalizations, applications for passports, and wills and administrations could be recorded here. You may wonder, "Why search here?" It could provide more clues. For example, when your great-grandfather died, he may have left a will stating that the house was to go to his wife and then to the children. If this was the case, each person would be named. You can identify other brothers and sisters of your grandfather or grandmother. A sister, if she was married, could be listed as Mary Ryan Kelly, wife of John Kelly. These data will give you clues about another branch of the family.

A deed will record when land was purchased and from whom. If the land was an inheritance, the deed will tell you who died and how the estate was settled. In one case, a researcher in Ireland could not locate any information on a

Records such as ships' passenger lists can provide details on your family's immigration to the United States. For some, such as the Casey family, shown above in 1929, the trip was bittersweet. While Bridget Casey was able to bring nine of her children with her to Connecticut to be reunited with their father, the second eldest child had to remain in Ireland after failing to pass the immigration test.

female ancestor. While looking at deeds in his county, he came across a deed stating that the land was being given to his great-great grandfather by a triple great-grandfather as part of the great-great-grandmother's dowry. This piece of information helped the researcher get back to the 1780s. Did your ancestor ever sue anyone or was he or she sued? These records will be found in your local courthouse. If your ancestor applied to become a citizen, there will be a court record of this event. All court cases should have documentation that can be found in the Hall of Records. These are just a few examples of the types of records that can be found.

The National Archives

The National Archives not only maintains census records, but also all documents that pertain to official events at a federal level. Immigration and naturalization lists, ships' passenger lists, military service records, pensions, and any federal court actions will end up at the National Archives. The different branches of the archives each have a specialty. For example, for ships' passenger records, try the Northeast Regional Branch located in New York City. There are guides available, and your library should have them. Check with your librarian. Consult the **Resources** at the end of this chapter to find the regional branches near you.

Other Sources of Information

Once you have exhausted the local library's resources, where else can you go to look for information? Historical societies at both the state and local level often have libraries with fine collections of personal papers, business records, and research done by individuals. Some will have indexes to historical periodicals. Some societies index local cemeteries, while others work on various projects to preserve and protect local history. These groups may also have clubs or seminars on conducting research or publishing a family history. They also provide the opportunity to talk with others who are working in the same area. Who knows—you may end up meeting a cousin!

Catholic church records in the United States may be useful in your research, but access to these records varies greatly. Some churches allow access to records that are more than 100 years old, for example, while others do not allow researchers to examine their records at all. It is best to contact directly the church your ancestor attended to find out whether they will allow you to search their records.

Family History Centers

The Church of Jesus Christ of Latter-day Saints, or the Mormons, have an extensive network of Family History Centers around the country. Genealogy is part of the mis-

Many Irish immigrants fought bravely in the American Civil War. This engraving shows Irish and German immigrants being recruited at Ellis Island to fight for their newly adopted country. Military records can provide important information on your ancestors who have served in the armed forces.

sion of the LDS Church, and they have gathered a vast amount of records, mainly vital records. They will provide them to visitors of Family History Centers. (You do not need to be a church member to use these facilities.) If you are interested in seeing what they have, check your telephone directory for the facility nearest you, or contact the Family History Library (FHL) in Salt Lake City, Utah (listed in the **Resources**). Most of the records are stored on microfilm. Materials that are not available at your local center can usually be borrowed from the main branch.

The Internet
The Internet provides a wealth of opportunities for genealogists. If you have access to a computer, a modem, and an Internet provider, you can take advantage of this tool. More

and more genealogists are sharing their work on the Internet, as well as using it to conduct research and to confirm information. Many organizations, libraries, and agencies have home pages on the Internet, from which you can browse their offerings and go on to other linked pages. Irish genealogy is one of the most actively discussed genealogical topics on the Internet, so you will have a lot of company. See the **Resources** for specific Internet sites that you shouldn't miss.

Resources

BEGINNING YOUR SEARCH

Allen, Desmond Walls, and Billingsley, Carolyn Earle.
Beginner's Guide to Family History Research. **Bountiful, UT: American Genealogical Lending Library, 1991.**

A fine introduction to family history research. Includes many examples and chapters on organization, utilization of specific archives and libraries, use of census and other records, and interviews and correspondence.

American Genealogy: A Basic Course. **National Genealogical Society.**

By writing to the National Genealogical Society at 4527 17th Street North, Arlington, VA 22207-2363, you can acquire a brochure about this program. It incorporates both written and video guides and is an excellent introduction to beginning your search.

Beard, Timothy F. *How to Find Your Family Roots.*
New York: McGraw-Hill, 1977.

This is an excellent source for the beginner. It describes the various types of records you will need to look at and shows you how to use them effectively.

Cooper, Kay. *Where Did You Get Those Eyes: A Guide to Discovering Your Family History.* **New York: Walker & Co., 1988.**

A thorough guide to researching your family history, from interviewing to researching in genealogical libraries. Reprinted as *Discover It Yourself: Where Did You Get Those Eyes?* (Avon, 1993.)

An Irish American Photo Album

North Channel

Londonderry · Antrim

Donegal

Londonderry

NORTHERN IRELAND (U.K.)

Donegal · Tyrone · Lough Neagh

Donegal Bay · Lower Lough Erne · U L S T E R · Belfast

Leitrim · Fermanagh · Down

North Atlantic Ocean

Upper Lough Erne · Armagh

Bangor Erris · Sligo · Monaghan

Lough Conn · Lough Allen · Cavan · Cavan

Mayo · Louth

Claremorris · Roscommon · Longford · Lough Sheelin

Lough Mask · Lough Ree · Meath · Irish Sea

Clifden · Tuam · Trim

Lough Corrib · Galway · Westmeath · Dublin · Dublin Bay

Galway · REPUBLIC OF IRELAND · Offaly · Tullamore · Liffey River · Dublin · Naas · Kildare

Port Laoise · Wicklow

Lough Derg · Laoighis

Ennistimon · Clare · Durrow · Arklow

Nenagh · Kilkenny · Carlow

Limerick · Tipperary · Kilkenny · Wexford

Limerick · Tipperary · Clonmel · Rosslare

Tralee · Mallow · Waterford · Waterford

Kerry · Cork · Saint George's Channel

Kenmare · Cork

Bantry

The Emerald Isle has given us a precious gift of its people and their ideas and talents. In fact, there was an Irishman on board Christopher Columbus' first voyage to the Americas. Irish Americans are one of the largest ethnic groups in the United States. One need only look through the list of U.S. presidents with Irish ancestry—Jackson, Polk, Buchanan, Arthur, McKinley, Wilson, Kennedy, Nixon, Reagan, and Clinton—to see the tremendous influence of Irish Americans on American politics. Likewise, the literary tradition, music, religion, and dance of Ireland have made a deep impression on the American cultural scene. Although the most famous wave of Irish immigration occurred after the failure of the potato crop in Ireland in 1845, Irish immigrants came to the United States by the thousands seeking new opportunities during most of the nineteenth century. They persevered in the face of anti-Irish and anti-Catholic discrimination and forged successful lives in their adopted country. The Irish continue to immigrate to the United States today, bringing their wit, warmth, and talent as their fellow Irish did before them. As one of the most established American ethnic groups, Irish Americans have become an inextricable part of American culture, past and present.

Bill Clinton proudly accepts the Irish American of the Year Award in New York on March 11, 1996. *Irish America* magazine publisher Niall O'Dowd and U.S. ambassador to Ireland Jean Kennedy Smith present the award while Senator Edward Kennedy looks on. Clinton was recognized by *Irish America* for his profound commitment to resolving the "Troubles," the term commonly used to refer to the conflict over control of Northern Ireland. The Clinton administration's unwavering support of the peace process in Ireland was a major factor behind the Irish Republican Army's cease-fire of August 31, 1994.

In November 1990, Mary Robinson became the first woman to be elected president of the Republic of Ireland. Throughout her distinguished political career, Robinson has been a staunch supporter of human rights and an inspiring leader. She has received numerous awards for academic excellence. Above, Robinson receives an honorary degree from Fordham University in New York on May 20, 1995, as Fordham President Father Joseph A. O'Hare looks on.

The picturesque mountains, glens, and coast of the Antrim district in Northern Ireland attract many tourists. Above, the ruins of Dunluce Castle, a Norman structure built in the thirteenth century by Richard de Burgh, Earl of Ulster, teeters on the edge of a cliff overlooking the Irish Sea. During a storm in 1639, the section of the castle containing the kitchens tumbled into the sea, drowning several cooks. The castle fell into decay after it was abandoned in the mid-seventeenth century.

The village of Blarney, in southwest Ireland, is the site of the famous Blarney Castle, constructed in the fifteenth century. According to Irish legend, those who kiss the Blarney Stone—an inscribed rock near the top of the castle—are endowed with powers of eloquence and persuasion.

Situated at the mouth of the River Lagan, Belfast (above) developed into a prosperous seaport and industrial center in the nineteenth century. Belfast became the capital of Northern Ireland in 1920 when the six Ulster counties were partitioned from the rest of Ireland. Belfast has been plagued by violent conflict between Roman Catholics and Protestants for over a century. Since the late 1970s, the city has made a concerted effort to improve its image by investing heavily in economic and cultural development.

Dublin is the capital and principal seaport of the Republic of Ireland. It is located on Dublin Bay, an inlet of the Irish Sea, at the mouth of the Liffey River. The Liffey bisects Dublin from east to west and is spanned by ten bridges. The most notable of these bridges is O'Connell's Bridge (seen here), which connects the main roads of Dublin. This bridge is named after Catholic political leader Daniel O'Connell, who in the early nineteenth century led efforts to repeal the severe Penal Laws against Irish Roman Catholics.

Millions of Irish Americans gather every year along Fifth Avenue in New York City for the oldest and largest St. Patrick's Day celebration in the United States. Many participants don traditional Irish costumes and play the bagpipes or the fiddle. Others dance an Irish jig, like these members of the Irish Dancing and Musicians Association. St. Patrick's Cathedral, the largest Roman Catholic church in the United States, can be seen in the background.

Irish-born soldiers fought valiantly in the Civil War on behalf of both the Union and Confederate armies. A quarter of all foreign-born volunteers in the Union Army were from Ireland. The famous Irish Brigade was originally comprised of the 63rd, 69th, and 88th New York infantry regiments. Above, participants carry the Irish Brigade flag in a 1990 reenactment of the Civil War's Battle of Belmont near Freeburg, Illinois. The battle, fought on November 7, 1861, was one of the first Civil War victories for soldiers under General Ulysses S. Grant, commander of the Union army.

Riverdance is a highly acclaimed spectacle that features elements of traditional Irish dance, music, and song. Performed by an international group of dancers, the show is a dynamic celebration of Irish culture that focuses on the evolution of Irish dance. *Riverdance* has been performed before sold-out audiences in London, Dublin, and New York City. Its widespread success has heightened public interest in Irish dance.

U2, one of the world's most popular rock bands, was formed in 1978 when its four members were still students at Dublin's Mount Temple school. U2's lyrics often comment on political issues, such as human rights and the conflict over Northern Ireland. The song "Sunday Bloody Sunday," for example, laments the ongoing violence in Northern Ireland. U2 has participated in numerous concerts in support of political and social causes around the world.

Irish American actor George Clooney has risen to prominence in the role of Dr. Douglas Ross on the popular television drama series *ER*. Clooney's work in *ER* earned him an Emmy nomination for best actor in 1995 and a Golden Globe nomination for best actor in 1996. Clooney has carried this success into a flourishing film career. He was included in *Irish America* magazine's 1996 list of the Top 100 Irish Americans.

Justice Sandra Day O'Connor had a distinguished career in the Arizona state legislature and later as a superior court judge in the same state. O'Connor was the first woman to be sworn in as a justice of the U.S. Supreme Court, in 1981.

Above, a scene from *Juno and the Paycock,* Sean O'Casey's 1924 drama about slum life in Dublin, is performed in New York City by members of the Irish Repertory Theatre. Founded in 1988, the Theatre is dedicated to bringing classic and contemporary works by Irish and Irish American playwrights to the American stage. In 1993, the Irish Repertory Theatre won the New York Drama Desk Award for Excellence in Presenting Distinguished Irish Drama. In the same year, the Theatre produced *Seconds Out,* a drama written by seven Irish teenagers, as part of its ongoing effort to attract young audiences.

Poet Seamus Heaney was born in Mossbawn, Northern Ireland. His native land has served as a rich source of inspiration for his poetry. Heaney's poignant and nonpartisan treatment of the violence in Northern Ireland has made him a cultural symbol of hope for peace in Ulster. Heaney has held prestigious academic posts at Oxford and Harvard universities and he was awarded the Nobel Prize in Literature in 1995. Above, Heaney is pictured in Dublin, where he has resided since 1976.

A breakthrough in the long-standing conflict over Northern Ireland was achieved when the Irish Republican Army (IRA) announced "a cessation of military operations" on August 31, 1994. But on February 9, 1996, violence erupted once again, to the dismay of the Irish populace. The resurgence of IRA terrorist campaigns has put the peace process in jeopardy. Above, children at a peace rally in the village of Dunboyne, County Meath, demonstrate for an end to violence and a return to peace. Thousands congregated at similar peace rallies throughout Northern Ireland and the Republic of Ireland to urge the IRA to resume its cease-fire and to save the imperiled peace process.

Doane, Gilbert. *Searching for Your Ancestors: The How and Why of Genealogy.* **New York: Bantam Books, 1974.**

This very readable book explains the techniques the researcher will need to employ for in-depth research. The chapters are geared to the casual reader. Includes chapters on finding information in cemeteries, county courthouses, government agencies, family papers, and churches. Contains appendixes on locating vital statistics, census records, and bibliographies.

Draznin, Yaffa. *The Family Historian's Handbook.* **New York: Jove, 1977.**

This book is for all hyphenated Americans. The author discusses problems you might encounter and offers techniques for research both in the United States and overseas.

Greenwood, Val D. *Researcher's Guide to American Genealogy*, **2d ed. Baltimore: Genealogical Publishing Co., 1990.**

This is the basic text for most of the home study courses offered by the National Genealogical Society and other organizations. A highly recommended genealogical guide that explains everything from getting started to intermediate-level researching. Also includes resources for more advanced research.

Hey, David. *The Oxford Guide to Family History.* **New York: Oxford University Press, 1993.**

Contains great chapters on searching government records and church registries. Also has information on the origin of particular family names.

Hilton, Suzanne. *Who Do You Think You Are? Digging for Your Family Roots.* **Philadelphia: Westminster Press, 1977.**

Although you will want to acquire more recent sources eventually, this book remains a good place to start your genealogical search. Written for young people.

Lackey, Richard S. *Cite Your Sources*. Baltimore: Genealogical Publishing Co., 1980.

The only thing worse than not finding the information you want is being unable to relocate it after you found it the first time. Learn how to identify your sources correctly and accurately and find them again when you need to.

Neagles, James C., and Neagles, Lila Lee. *Locating Your Immigrant Ancestor*. Salt Lake City: Everton Publishers, 1986.

This reference book for naturalization records will assist you in locating the documentation you need. This text can save you both time and energy.

Parker, Kenneth B. *Find Your Roots: A Beginner's Kit for Tracing Your Family Tree*. Southfield, MI: Lezell-Brasch Associates, 1977.

A great tool for young or beginning genealogists. Includes sample pedigree charts and family group sheets for you to photocopy or use as a model when creating your own.

Schreiner-Yantis, Netti. *Genealogical and Local History Books in Print*, 4th ed. 3 vols. Springfield, VA: Schreiner-Yantis, 1990.

These volumes contain information on genealogical publications, supplies, and services. The author also runs a genealogical supply company.

Westin, Jeane Eddy. *Finding Your Roots: How Every American Can Trace His Ancestors—At Home and Abroad*. New York: Ballantine Books, 1977.

Covers everything from how to use the most fundamental records to writing and publishing family history. Contains a list of archives and stores that specialize in genealogical research.

Wright, Norman E. *Preserving Your American Heritage.* **Provo, UT: Brigham Young University Press, 1981.**

This is a convincing argument on why you should trace your family history in the United States. Gives you a sense of the richness and complexity of the American heritage.

FAMILY GROUP SHEETS AND PEDIGREE CHARTS

Evelyn Spears Family Group Sheet Exchange
East 12502 Frideger
Elk, WA 99009

A service that provides previously researched family group sheets from a catalog of 14,000. The charge for each surname you request is about ten dollars.

Genealogical Center, Inc.
International Family Group Sheet Exchange
P.O. Box 17698
Tampa, FL 33682

You can write and request their catalog of over 8,000 surnames. The service charges thirty cents per page of researched data, and studies can range from ten to 300 pages.

Schreiner-Yantis Family Group Sheets
GBIP
6818 Lois Drive
Springfield, VA 22150

Designed by Netti Schreiner-Yantis, these family group sheets, pedigree charts, and other forms are widely considered the finest available. Write for a catalog and price list.

NAMES

Bell, Robert. *The Book of Ulster Surnames*. **Belfast: Blackstaff Press, 1988.**

A reference book listing family names of Ulster province, and where they came from.

Camp, Anthony. *Everyone Has Roots*. **Baltimore: Genealogical Publishing Co., 1978.**

This book is a general introduction to genealogical researching, but it is notable for its information about surnames, particularly in the British Isles.

Hanks, Patricia, and Hodges, Flavia. *A Dictionary of First Names*. **New York: Oxford University Press, 1990.**

An excellent source on determining whether a relative's name is of Irish origin. A study of over 4,500 European and American names, usually including the non-English form of the name.

————. *A Dictionary of Surnames*. **New York: Oxford University Press, 1989.**

A study of the origins of over 100,000 common surnames and their European origin. Especially helpful in discovering whether a name is of more than one national origin.

MacLysaght, Edward. *The Surnames of Ireland*, **6th ed. Dublin: Irish Academic Press, 1991.**

A comprehensive listing of Irish surnames, along with variant spellings of those names, and where the family originated.

Noble, Wilfred Vernon. *Nicknames: Past and Present*. **London: H. Hamilton, 1976.**

Having a working knowledge of historical nicknames can help you interpret letters, diaries, and other personal writings of your family members. Also explains how nicknames can turn into surnames.

Smith, Elsdon C. *American Surnames.* **Baltimore: Genealogical Publishing Co., 1969.**

Explains the roots and meanings of different surnames and their derivatives. Covers most ethnic, religious, and geographic surnames.

Woulfe, Rev. Patrick. *Irish Names and Surnames.* **Baltimore: Genealogical Publishing Co., 1993.**

First printed in 1923, this book includes an informative history of Irish names and a dictionary of thousands of names, their meanings, English equivalents, and regions of origin in Ireland. The section on clan names is especially useful for genealogists.

CENSUS RECORDS

Lainhart, Ann S. *State Census Records.* **Baltimore: Genealogical Publishing Co., 1992.**

Obtaining census records is essential to your genealogical project. This is the first published comprehensive list of state census records.

Thorndale, William, and Dollarhide, William. *Map Guide to the U.S. Federal Censuses: 1790–1920.* **Baltimore: Genealogical Publishing Co., 1991.**

Displays the U.S. county boundaries from 1790 to 1920. Also includes keys to finding census records within a particular area and an index listing all present-day counties.

MILITARY RECORDS

Johnson, Lt. Col. Richard S. *How to Locate Anyone Who Is or Has Been in the Military.* **San Antonio, TX: MIE Publishing, 1993.**

Contains addresses and phone numbers of offices containing relevant military documents. Includes tips for locating relatives who have served in the military.

PASSENGER RECORDS

Colletta, John P. *They Came in Ships*. **Salt Lake City: Ancestry, Inc., 1989.**

This small book describes what kind of information can be found in passenger records, the specifics of passenger records from various time periods, and how to find the records of your own ancestors. Includes a well-annotated bibliography of useful sources.

Filby, P. William, ed. *Passenger & Immigration Lists Index: A Reference Guide to Published Lists of About 500,000 Passengers Who Arrived in America in the 17th, 18th, and 19th Centuries*. **3 vols. Detroit: Gale Research Co., 1981.**

A comprehensive guide to passenger lists of immigrant ships from the seventeenth through nineteenth centuries.

Filby, P. William, and Meyer, Mary K., eds. *Supplement to Passenger & Immigration Lists*. **Detroit: Gale Research Co., 1987.**

An update and supplement to the above volumes.

Hackett, J. Dominick, and Early, Charles M. *Passenger Lists from Ireland*. **Baltimore: Clearfield Company, 1994.**

Lists some 5,150 passengers who sailed from Ireland to the United States in the years 1811 and 1815–1816. The name of the ship, date of arrival, port of departure, port of entry, and point of origin are given for each passenger.

McDonnell, Frances. *Emigrants from Ireland to America 1735–1743*. **Baltimore: Genealogical Publishing Co., 1992.**

Taken from the *Journal of the House of Commons/Kingdom of Ireland*, this is a list of 2,000 felons and vagabonds who were forcibly transported from Ireland during these years. (Often, these people were in prison for stealing food.) The lists include name, place, reason for deportation, and sometimes the ship and destination of deportees.

Mitchell, Brian. *Irish Emigration Lists 1833–39.* **Balti-more: Genealogical Publishing Co., 1989.**

Lists of names and personal data taken from the ordinance survey memoirs for Counties Londonderry and Antrim.

———. *Irish Passenger Lists 1847–1871: Lists of Passengers Sailing from Londonderry to America on Ships of the J. & J. Cooke Line and the McCorkell Line.* **Baltimore: Genealogical Publishing Co., 1988.**

Check this source if you have reason to believe that your ancestors immigrated during this time period.

O'Brien, Michael J. *The Irish in America: Immigration, Land, Probate, Administrations, Birth, Marriage and Burial Records of the Irish in America in and about the Eighteenth Century.* **Baltimore: Clearfield Company, 1990.**

Contains two passenger lists: one of nearly 500 names of Irish immigrants to New England between 1716 and 1769, and the other of 1,000 who came to Virginia between 1623 and 1666.

Tepper, Michael. *American Passenger Records: A Guide to the Records of Immigrants Arriving at American Ports by Sail and Steam.* **Baltimore: Genealogical Publishing Co., 1993.**

Gives examples of passenger lists and instructions on how to use them. Covers records from the Colonial period to the twentieth century.

VITAL RECORDS

Kemp, Thomas J. *Vital Records Handbook.* **Baltimore: Genealogical Publishing Co., 1988.**

Tells the cost of obtaining vital records, such as birth, death, and marriage certificates. Also includes copies of the state forms for requesting vital records. Well organized, with alphabetical arrangement by state and addresses and phone numbers.

Where to Write for Vital Records: Births, Deaths, Marriages and Divorces. **Superintendent of Documents, U.S. Government Printing Office, Washington, DC 20402.**

Provides valuable assistance in obtaining and utilizing vital records, both from the government and from source books.

HISTORICAL AND GENEALOGICAL ORGANIZATIONS

American Irish Historical Society
991 Fifth Avenue
New York, NY 10028

The Historical Society has a library with over 10,000 volumes on Irish and Irish American subjects. Their collections of papers cover topics such as the history of the Irish in America.

Family History Library (FHL)
35 North West Temple Street
Salt Lake City, UT 84150

This is the largest genealogical library in the world. Its holdings include microfilm versions of censuses, parish registers, published family histories, vital records, atlases, and many other sources. Write for a list of local Family History Centers.

National Genealogical Society
4527 17th Street North
Arlington, VA 22207-2399
703-525-0050

This organization provides a clearinghouse for the genealogist by setting standards for excellence, developing programs to increase the knowledge of its members, and providing a library for research. While this is geared more to the professional than the novice, the journals and newsletters are a good source of current information and techniques.

NATIONAL ARCHIVES AND NATIONAL ARCHIVES REGIONAL BRANCHES

**National Archives
Washington, DC 20408
202-501-5240**

This is the repository for all federal documents, including census records, ships' passenger lists, military pension applications, and federal court proceedings. The main archive is located in Washington, DC, but there are regional branches throughout the country. Each branch is responsible for a specific area of interest. There is an excellent guide to help you learn about researching in the archives. It can be found in a good reference collection in the public library. Write or call for a list of free publications and information on the regional branches.

Central Plains
**2312 East Bannister Road
Kansas City, MO 64131
816-926-6272**

Contains information on Iowa, Kansas, Missouri, Nebraska.

Great Lakes
**7358 South Pulaski Road
Chicago, IL 60629
312-581-7816**

Contains information on Illinois, Indiana, Michigan, Minnesota, Ohio, Wisconsin.

Mid-Atlantic
Ninth and Market Streets
Philadelphia, PA 19107
215-597-3000

Contains information on Delaware, Maryland, Pennsylvania, Virginia, West Virginia.

New England
380 Trapelo Road
Waltham, MA 02154
617-647-8100

Contains information on Connecticut, Maine, Massachusetts, New Hampshire, Rhode Island, Vermont.

Northeast
Building 22—MOT Bayonne
Bayonne, NJ 07002-5388
201-823-7252

Contains information on New Jersey, New York, Puerto Rico, Virgin Islands.

Pacific Northwest
6125 Sand Point Way NE
Seattle, WA 98115
206-526-6507

Contains information on Alaska, Idaho, Oregon, Washington state.

Pacific Sierra
1000 Commodore Drive
San Bruno, CA 94066
415-876-9009

Contains information on Hawaii, Nevada, northern California.

Pacific Southwest
24000 Avila Road
Mailing address: P.O. Box 6719

Laguna Niguel, CA 92677-6719
714-643-4241

Contains information on Arizona, southern California, Nevada's Clark County.

Rocky Mountain
Building 48, Denver Federal Center
Denver, CO 80225
303-236-0818

Contains information on Colorado, Montana, North Dakota, South Dakota, Utah, Wyoming.

Southeast Region
1557 St. Joseph Avenue
East Point, GA 30344
404-763-7474 or 763-7477

Contains information on Alabama, Florida, Georgia, Kentucky, Mississippi, North Carolina, South Carolina, Tennessee.

Southwest
501 West Felix Street
Mailing address: P.O. Box 6216
Fort Worth, TX 76115
817-334-5525

Contains information on Arkansas, Louisiana, New Mexico, Oklahoma, Texas.

INTERNET WEB SITES

Everton Publishers Genealogy Page
http://www.everton.com

This page contains information on getting started as well as specific information on ethnic, religious, and social groups. Includes an online edition of the genealogical magazine *Everton's Genealogical Helper* and provides links to archives, libraries, and other Internet resources.

Genealogy Home Page
ftp://ftp.cac.psu.edu/pub/genealogy
http://ftp.cac.psu.edu/~saw/genealogy.html

By filling out the survey linked to this home page, you will be granted access to many genealogical links, allowing you to communicate with other genealogists, search new databases, and order genealogical software online.

LDS Research Guides
ftp://hipp.etsu.edu/pub/genealogy

This site focuses on the Research Outline Guides produced by the Family History Library in Salt Lake City. Subjects include getting started, frequently asked genealogy questions, and techniques for photograph dating.

National Archives and Records Administration
gopher://gopher.nara.gov
http://www.nara.gov

NARA is the government agency responsible for managing the records of the federal government. Through this page you can find the location and business hours for regional archives or access information on finding and using particular government documents.

U.S. Census Bureau
ftp://gateway.census.gov
http://www.census.gov

From this site you can access statistics about population, housing, economy, and geography as compiled by the U.S. Department of Commerce Bureau of the Census. You can also conduct specific word searches according to subject or geographic location.

Utah State Archives Hotlinks: Genealogical Resources
http://utstdp.www.state.ut.us/~archives/referenc/
!genealo.htm

This extensive web site has links to genealogical resources on the Internet, genealogical databases and libraries, and commercial services. Also provides useful links to searching for places and living people.

World Wide Web Genealogy Demo Page
http://demo.genweb.org/gene/genedemo.html

This page is still under construction, but its goal is to "create a coordinated, interlinked, distributed worldwide genealogy database." Even in its incomplete form, GenWeb allows you to access all known genealogical databases searchable through the www.

WEB SITES OF SPECIAL INTEREST

An Scathan
http://www.underbridge.com/anscathan/index.htm

An Scathan (The Mirror) is "the prime information provider to the Celtic community in America." Offers a publication covering topics such as arts and entertainment, business news, and fiction.

Ancestral Videos
http://www.cis.ie/marketplace/AV

Based in Cork, Ireland, this company can provide you with a video version of your Irish roots. Contact them via the Internet or by phone (353-21-889422) for information about acquiring a video record of your Irish forebears.

County Tipperary Historical Society
http://www.iol.ie/~tipplibs/Welcome.htm

The historical society encourages new research on the history, archaeology, folklore, and geography of County Tipperary. You will certainly want to check out this site if your relatives came from this county in Ireland. Includes links to the *Tipperary Historical Journal*, newsletters, and mailbox.

Flyleaf
http://www.adnet.ie/clients/flyleaf.html

The homepage for Flyleaf Press, a publisher of family history guides and references. Many of their works are standards for Irish family history research, and they are constantly creating new publications to meet changing needs.

Genealogical Research in Ireland
http://pwaldron.bess.ted.ie/roots_ie.htm

A great resource for tracing your Irish family history in Ireland.

Government of Ireland
http://www.irlgov.ie/

This site has its own search engine that you can use to research specific topics. It also provides a list of Irish organizations and information on Ireland, which may be useful if you are planning a visit there.

Historic Publications
http://www.iol.ie/~histpub

A non-profit organization that provides a general description of the history of Irish and British surnames. Each history is printed on textured parchment paper and is available for a small fee.

House of Names
http://egi-bin.iol.ie/shopping/houseofnames

The House of Names online brochure. Supplies coats of arms and heraldic products by mail order.

Index to *Irish Genealogy Guide*
http://www.bess.ted.ie/roots/prototyp/links.htm

A massive source to help you get the information you need from the *Irish Genealogy Guide*. Covers everything from "Abbreviations Used in the System" to "Wills and Grant Books."

Irish American Partnership
http://www.adnet.ie/iap/tourist.htm

Initiated by the Irish Tourist Board, this partnership was meant to continue the growth of tourism in Ireland. Excellent resource for information on traveling to the birthplaces or homes of your Irish ancestors.

Irish Family History Foundation
http://www.mayo-ireland.ie/roots.htm

The Irish Family History Foundation is the coordinating body for a network of government-approved genealogical research centers in the Republic of Ireland and Northern Ireland. The web site provides tips on starting your research and on topics such as Irish names, and describes records sources and the services offered by the centers.

Irish Genealogical Foundation
http://www.tyrell.net/~ireland1/

This web site describes the activities of the foundation, such as free surname listing and surname research and the organizing of small group trips to Ireland for those in search of their roots. From this site you can also access information on the foundation's journal of Irish families and a catalog of its family history books.

IRLGEN: Tracing Your Irish Ancestors
http://www.bess.ted.ie/roots//prototyp/genweb2.htm

. Focuses on doing genealogical research in Ireland, although it covers many other areas as well. Aims to "lead you to the record-keepers who hold the paper records of greatest relevance to your search."

IRLNET
http://wombatix.iol.ie/ir/net

Database featuring over 900 resources on different aspects of Irish culture, both in Ireland and abroad. Among the many links featured on this page besides genealogy are culture, politics, and history.

National Archives of Ireland—Family History and Genealogy

http://147.252.133.152/nat-arch/genealogy.html

Guide to the National Archives of Ireland for people beginning their family history research. After reading the information in this document, you will be better prepared to speak with a reading room staff member about acquiring information on your family.

North of Ireland Family History Society
http://www.os.pub.ac.uk/nifhs/

Provides many links for learning more about the organization, researching your Northern Ireland roots, and accessing related sites on the World Wide Web. Also has history and tourist information.

Ulster Historical Foundation
http://www.ireland.net/marketplace/uhf

Founded in 1956, this non-profit organization promotes the history and genealogy of Ulster, in Northern Ireland. Access a number of UHL and related publications from this Internet site.

IRISH AMERICAN PUBLICATIONS

These publications will help you keep up to date on Irish and Irish American people and events. Watch for articles on topics related to genealogy.

Boston Irish Reporter
304 Neponset Avenue
Dorchester, MA 02122

The Desert Shamrock
1801 S. Jentilly Lane, Suite B-12
Tempe, AZ 85281-5738

Irish America Magazine
P.O. Box 209
Pearl River, NY 10965

Irish American News
503 South Oak Park Avenue, Suite 204
Oak Park, IL 60303

The Irish American Post
301 N. Water Street
Milwaukee, WI 53202

The Irish Echo
309 Fifth Avenue
New York, NY 10016

The Irish Edition
803 East Willow Grove Avenue
Wyndmoor, PA 19038-7907

Irish Eye
c/o Masterpiece Publications, Inc.
15414 N. 7th St.
Suite 8, Box 176
Phoenix, AZ 85022

Irish News
P.O. Box 1257
Santa Monica, CA 90406-1257

The Irish Voice
P.O. Box 686
Sikerville, NJ 08081-9905

San Francisco Gael
2403 Ocean Avenue
San Francisco, CA 94127

San Francisco Irish Herald
2123 Market Street
San Francisco, CA 94114

Chapter 4
Researching in Ireland

Traveling to Ireland to research your family history may not seem like a very realistic goal right now, especially if you are a student without an income of your own. You might plan this trip as a long-term goal, after you have done all the research you can about the history of your family in the United States. If your family is already planning a trip to Ireland, of course, you can try to incorporate your research into the itinerary. Or, your family may become so caught up in the excitement of your project that they change their theme park vacation plans and make Ireland their new destination!

If you are committed to the idea of traveling to Ireland and studying Irish history and culture, as well as the history of your own family, you might consider participating in a study-abroad program, either at the high school or college level. Talk with your school counselor or study-abroad office.

Genealogy-inspired trips, or "ethnic tourism," to Ireland are a growing trend among Irish Americans, many of whom are looking back on their Irish roots with a new sense of discovery and pride. Former U.S. President Ronald Reagan, using a professional genealogist, traced his family back to County Tipperary. In 1961, the actress Grace Kelly visited her grandfather's former farm in County Mayo, and many other Americans have followed her example by returning to Ireland to visit their ancestral homes.

The Irish government is very encouraging of trips by Irish Americans interested in their heritage. In 1992, the tourist board held a month-long Homecoming Festival, featuring genealogical seminars as well as cultural events.

Many Irish Americans, seeking to learn more about their ancestors, travel to Ireland to explore their roots. The actress Grace Kelly, Princess of Monaco, sparked an increase in this trend in 1960 when she returned to the house where her grandfather was born in County Mayo. Ellen Mulgrone, the tiny thatched cottage's resident, stepped out to fetch some water and was snapped by photographers.

For information on travel to Ireland, contact the Irish Tourist Board at 345 Park Avenue, New York, NY 10154; 212-418-0800.

The dream of all of us who are searching for our Irish ancestors is to locate the place they came from. Be it a little cottage or a large estate, it is part of why we began our search. This chapter will examine the techniques and sources you will need to employ to find your ancestral home.

The Office of the General Registrar

The office of the General Registrar in Dublin is commonly known as Joyce House, and it contains all vital records for Ireland starting in 1864. There are Church of Ireland (the

Anglican Church) marriage records starting in 1845. Birth, death, and marriage records are indexed separately. Each index lists the person's name, the registration district, and the volume and page number on which the record appears. These indexes are arranged by quarter so you must look in four sections to check the entire year. In the back of each index you will discover late and foreign registrations. To get an actual copy of the record, you will have to fill out the forms and pay a fee. Try to be as accurate as possible in requesting information or it could become expensive. One advantage to using this office is that you can search all of Ireland from one location and get the records in a reasonable amount of time.

The birth record will contain the date of birth, the child's name, parents' names (including the mother's maiden name), the place of residence, and the informant (the source of the information). The marriage record lists the bride and groom, their ages, residences (townland), fathers' names, parents' marital status, the occupation of the groom as well as that of both fathers, the witnesses, the parish in which it took place, the date, and the minister who performed the ceremony. Death records list the name, date, place, marital status, cause of death, and the informant, but no additional family data, which is disappointing to genealogists.

If your family left Ireland after 1864, these records are worth investigating. The Family History Centers of the LDS Church have the indexes on microfilm so you can do some of this work in the United States, but to get the actual records you will have to write Ireland. You can get the official certificate or just a copy from the microfilm. The copy will in many cases have your ancestors' signatures or some additional information.

The National Library of Ireland

The National Library of Ireland in Dublin contains both printed materials and manuscripts relating to the history of Ireland. Books of gravestone inscriptions, newspapers, local histories, journals, directories, and a wealth of other printed information are available here. Visiting researchers must register, so bring your passport for identification. Once registered, go upstairs and start by using the catalogs. The library has a book catalog and a card catalog which are arranged by subject and author.

Microfilmed copies of Catholic Church parish registers containing baptismal, marriage, and, in some cases, burial records, are available on microfilm. There may be some restrictions on accessing these records, however. To use parish records you will need to locate the church your family attended. In many cases it will have the same name as the civil parish. Unlike American parishes, where the name of the parish is the same name as the church (St. Patrick's, St. Michael's, for example) a church in Ireland is called by a saint's name, but the parish is not. For the most part, these records are not indexed and may be written in either English or Latin. Some bishops have put limitations on the use of their records. Once you identify your family's parish, it is wise to write the bishop to see if there are any restrictions on parish records.

Before using parish registers, write down your family name and then misspell it as many different ways as you can. Then get your friends to do the same. This will help you to come up with the possible variations by which your family name may be listed. In the 1800s, spelling was not standardized and family names were easily misspelled. In one case, Honoria O'Brien, who married James Peters, had five children born in Ireland. Each was baptized in the same parish in County Tipperary. The father was listed as Jas. Peters (Jas. is a standard abbreviation for James). Honoria was listed as Nano Brian, Nano O'Brien, Honoria Bryan, Honoria O'Brian, and Nano Brien. The local priest knew the family well, so he had occasionally listed her by her nickname. The surname was spelled in a variety of ways.

You will notice in baptismal registers that a child's godparents are not usually a married couple. There are two reasons for this. First, it provided the child with ties to more than one family in the community. Second, the child had

As you conduct your research using Irish sources, you will need to know the name of the place where your ancestors lived. William Russell Grace, the financier, emigrated from Queenstown, Ireland. The W. R. Grace Company expanded its business worldwide, and Grace became the first Roman Catholic mayor of New York City in 1880.

two different sets of people who could provide for it in case something happened to the parents. This custom is found in many societies where economic hardship is a common feature of life.

The National Library manages a large manuscript collection of estate records. The information in it is not indexed, but if you can locate your ancestor and if he lived on one of these estates, there may be references to him and to the events surrounding his life in Ireland. Many of the landlords of Irish estates lived in England, so they hired agents or managers to run the estates for them. These people would make notes and reports to the owners about the crops, the weather, and anything else that would affect the estate.

The Genealogical Office

The Genealogical Office in Dublin provides some help as a consulting service. They can suggest sources for research and provide a list of reputable researchers. This is also the office of the Chief Herald (the office responsible for granting and confirming official coats of arms), and it operates a heraldic museum. There are some manuscripts in the museum which contain research on specific families, but these tend to be focused on the landed gentry rather than the common Irishman.

The National Archives of Ireland

The National Archives in Dublin was formerly the Public Record Office of Ireland. A fire during the civil war in 1922 destroyed many of the records in this office, but the indexes to many of the records still exist. The census records for 1901 and 1911 are available, but they are not indexed. There are other records similar to the census, and the originals of these records can be found here. Court records, along with wills and administrations, are part of this collection. All official records for Ireland can be found at the National Archives.

The Registry of Deeds

Deeds are kept at the Registry of Deeds located at the

King's Inn on Henrietta Street in Dublin. A deed is a record of a purchase of land. All deeds from 1708 and thereafter are here. There are two indexes to the deeds. One is by place name and the other is by grantor (the seller of the land). Professional genealogists in Ireland are working to create an index of grantees (the buyers of the land) but this is still in an early stage. If your family acquired land during the 1870s to 1880s, you may be able to locate a deed. If the family was wealthy, they may have owned properties in many counties, and a visit to the Registry of Deeds could prove very fruitful. When land is sold, the grantor must tell how he or she acquired the property. This information may provide clues to more of your family history.

Research in Northern Ireland

If your family is from Northern Ireland, then you will need to go to Belfast. Records for the pre-1920 period have been transferred to the Public Record Office of Northern Ireland. Duplicates of the pre-1920 information are in Dublin. For all information on the six counties (Londonderry, Antrim, Down, Armagh, Fermanagh, and Tyrone) after 1920, you will need to contact this office. The facility is set up just like the National Archives of Ireland, except that with only six counties, they have made indexing of these records a priority.

The Ulster Historical Foundation in Belfast, the non-profit public service arm of the Public Record Office of Northern Ireland, has indexed many of the records and made them available in various publications. They have researchers available to help you with your work.

The Irish Genealogical Project

The Irish Genealogical Project was created to help train young people to use computers. Heritage Centers were set up to gather materials that were then logged into computers. Staff began to index records and provide family history information to the many visitors to Ireland. The project began by indexing church records, graveyard records, and other local documents. The centers now provide that information for a fee. The Irish Tourist Board in New York can supply you with a list of the centers. Some centers provide full services, while others are still in the beginning stages. The quality and cost of records will vary, but Heritage Centers are becoming a major asset to the family historian.

Resources You Do Not Want to Miss

The famine in Ireland and the need to provide for the care of the poor resulted in the Poor Law Union, which required local governments to assist the poor. Taxing the local people was the only way to provide for the poor. Many documents useful to today's genealogists were generated by the taxation system. One of the first questions you are likely to be asked if you visit a records office in Ireland is "Have you used Griffith's *Valuation?*" This is officially named the *Primary Valuation of Ireland*, and it consists of a collection of printed valuation books, one for each barony or poor law union. Each book contains information about heads of households and their land for the period 1848 to 1864. You will find the name of the head of the household, the amount of land, the types of buildings, and the relative value of the holding. Copies of the *Primary Valuation* are available in major libraries and record offices in Ireland. The National Library holds indexes of the *Primary Valuation* by surname.

The National Library also holds the *Tithe Books*. The *Tithe Applotment Books* recorded the amount of tax paid in 1832 to support the Church of Ireland. This tax had to be paid by all Irish citizens even if they belonged to another religion. If you are lucky, you may be able to locate your ancestor and the exact place where he lived. If your ancestor shows up in the *Tithe Books* but not in Griffith's, he may have already left Ireland by 1848. If you have a unique name, there may only be two or three places where that name occurs and you can limit your searching to those areas.

After the first valuation, the Valuation Office was established in Dublin. Its purpose was to record all land transactions. The *Canceled Land Books* recorded this information, and you can use them to help identify the date of death of an ancestor or his or her date of emigration. The *Canceled Land Books* can be found at the Valuation Office, the address of which is in the **Resources**.

The Ordnance Survey maps provide a detailed look at the counties of Ireland. They were drawn in the 1830s and are very detailed. They show every road, church, village, and farm, as well as large estates. In many cases, the maps include the names of the families living in the houses or on the farms. Once you identify your ancestor's county, look at the map and you may be able to locate the house. The current Ordnance Survey Office is located in Phoenix Park in Dublin.

The *Alphabetical Index to the Townlands and Towns of Ireland* provides map references, the size in acres, the county, barony, civil parish, and the Poor Law Union district of each town. If your family lore has it that grandfather came from a specific town, you can use this index to find its exact location.

Local histories and journals should not be overlooked. They can provide you with local information that will not be available anywhere else. If you have access to the Internet, you can search the library catalogs of a number of American and Irish colleges and universities for specific titles. Use the name of the town or the county as a search word. Your local librarian can then locate and order the materials for you using interlibrary loan if they are not available at your library.

Irish Traditions That Help Genealogists

The Irish, like many other cultures, have a number of traditions that can help us with our research.

In many Irish families, the name of the first son is usually the name of the paternal grandfather. The second son often bears the name of the maternal grandfather. In the United States during the twentieth century, this tradition has been modified. The first-born son may have the names of both grandfathers—paternal first, and then maternal. John Joseph,

Gravestones, both in the United States and Ireland, can reveal important information about your ancestors. Above, a visitor to the ruins of the Seven Churches of Athlone examines the oldest intact Celtic cross, erected in memory of King Flann in 1014 AD.

Francis Patrick, and James Michael are a few examples of names from this tradition.

Irish godparents are usually related to the godchild's parents. Brothers, sisters, cousins, and in-laws are likely to be godparents, but seldom a married couple or a person of the grandparents' generation. If you can find out the relationship of the godparents, you may have located another branch of your family. The pallbearers at a funeral are usually close family—nephews, cousins, in-laws—or close family friends.

Is there a family story of a family member entering the religious life as a priest or a nun? When professing their vows, they were required to list their parents (including mother's maiden name), and the parish in which they were baptized. Parish records have been kept since before the civil registration began in 1864, so by locating a specific parish you may be able to find your great-grandfather's baptismal record and estimate when he was born.

Visit the cemeteries where your family members are buried. People do not want to be forgotten. With a little luck, you may be able to locate the graves of other relatives near those of your family. The gravestone may tell you where in Ireland they came from, who erected the stone, and, for women, their maiden names.

Problems You Might Encounter

The first problem you might encounter is that all the records for your immigrant ancestors say simply that they came from Ireland without naming a city or county. The Irish wanted to make new lives for themselves and were proud to become American citizens. In official documents, many chose not to dwell on the specifics of where they had come from.

You may be looking for a family of Ryans, O'Briens, or Kellys and you can't sort them out because all the first names are the same. Keep trying—go back over your completed research for other clues.

Let's say that you are back to 1830 and are stuck. That may be as far back as you can go. The records prior to 1850 are few, and those that do exist tend to focus on the wealthy.

Perhaps you have always heard that your ancestor was in the Irish army. This is not as good of a clue as it might seem, because until 1922 there was no Irish army. There were secret societies trying to overthrow British control of Ireland, and those groups did not keep records for obvious reasons. If your ancestor was really a soldier, then he would have joined the British or American military. If it was a British unit, then the records will be in London.

Do not get discouraged. Instead of looking for earlier ancestors, try looking for other family branches, such as the brothers and sisters of your immigrant ancestor.

Focus on what you have accomplished, and on putting your work together in a form that other relatives can enjoy and learn from. The last chapter of this book will help you to focus on your final presentation.

Resources

GENEALOGICAL SOURCES IN THE REPUBLIC OF IRELAND

The Genealogical Office
2 Kildare Street
Dublin 2, Ireland
Telephone: 011-353-1-618811
Fax: 011-353-1-676669

> The Consulting Service of this office will supply information on how to do your family history as well as a list of professional genealogists who can do the work for a fee. The main function of this office is heraldic in nature, and it researches and grants coats of arms as well as approves company logos.

National Archives of Ireland
Bishop Street
Dublin 8, Ireland
Telephone: 011-353-1-783711

> Formerly the Public Record Office of Ireland, this agency preserves the official documents of the country, such as census returns, wills, administrations, and all court proceedings. The move to Bishop Street has increased the size of the reading room and permitted more microform readers to be added.

The National Library of Ireland
Kildare Street
Dublin 2, Ireland
Telephone: 011-353-1-618811
Fax: 011-353-1-676669

> This research library for Ireland collects everything Irish

or of Irish interest. Books, newspapers, maps, periodicals, and some manuscript records make up this unique collection. The main reading room is open to the public, but you must register and bring your user's card each time you use the library. You will want to look for materials in the author or subject indexes. Do not forget to check the eleven-volume Hayes Catalog for manuscript and periodical information. The library has been working to gather newspapers from all over Ireland, microfilm them for preservation purposes, and then provide a list of their holdings for the researcher. If you are looking for a picture of the village your ancestor came from, the library has over 40,000 negatives from its collection of photographs on microfilm. These can be viewed in the reading room. Also available here are the indexes to the *Primary Valuation*.

Office of the General Registrar
Joyce House
8–11 Lombard Street
Dublin 2, Ireland
Telephone: 011-353-1-711000

All births, deaths, and marriages beginning in 1864 are recorded here. There are also some Church of Ireland marriages starting in 1845. The records for the six counties of Northern Ireland begin in 1864 and end in 1922. This is a working office, so the Irish mother who needs her child's birth certificate for school registration is as likely to be here as the genealogist. There is a fee to use the indexes as well as a fee for all copies of the records. There is a small research area. The advantage of working here is that all of the records for the entire country are housed in one spot. Address all inquiries to the director.

Ordnance Survey Office
Phoenix Park
Dublin 8, Ireland

This office holds detailed maps of Ireland's counties.

Registry of Deeds
King's Inn
Henrietta Street
Dublin 7, Ireland
Telephone: 011-353-1-733300

Since 1708 deeds of land in Ireland have been recorded in this office. There are indexes arranged by location and grantor (seller). During the eighteenth and nineteenth centuries, the deeds were only for the Protestant landowners, but with the Land League in the 1870s, Catholics were allowed to purchase land, and this information is now recorded. Leases, marriage settlements, mortgages, and other liens on property are described in the deed. There is a small fee to use the books and a fee to get a copy of any deeds you locate.

Representative Church Body Library
Braemor Park
Rathgar
Dublin 14, Ireland
Telephone: 011-353-1-979979

This library collects information on the Church of Ireland and its ministers. As a church closes, it is supposed to send its registers, vestry books, minute books, and any other records here. If you are looking for information about a minister or someone who worked on his property, this is a place to try. This collection is largely unindexed, and there is an excellent but small staff.

State Paper Office
Dublin Castle
Dublin 2, Ireland

Here are housed the records of the Uprising of 1798, convict ledgers, and other legal proceedings which transported convicts to Australia and America.

Valuation Office
6 Ely Place
Dublin 2, Ireland

This office was established to keep records of land holdings and their value. Among the useful records in this office are the *Cancelled Land Books*.

GENEALOGICAL SOURCES IN NORTHERN IRELAND

General Register Office
Oxford House
49–55 Chichester Street
Belfast BT1 4HL, Northern Ireland
Telephone: 011-0232-661621

The office is organized just like the Office of the General Registrar in Dublin. It has all of the originals of the vital records for the six counties from 1864 to today.

Linen Hall Library
17 Donegall Square North
Belfast BT1 5DG, Northern Ireland

The genealogy collection of this library focuses on the six counties and is open to the public. This library was part of the Belfast Reading Society's Library, but with the increased interest in genealogical research, it was moved to this separate facility.

Public Record Office of Northern Ireland
66 Balmoral Avenue
Belfast BT9 6NY, Northern Ireland

This office contains all of the original deeds, wills, administrations, and court proceedings from 1922 to the present as well as copies of the original records for the six counties.

GENEALOGICAL SOCIETIES

This is a small sample of the societies and clubs available to the genealogist. Many of these groups offer publications, workshops, classes, and seminars in addition to regular meetings. Another benefit is networking and having the opportunity to meet others researching in the same area or the same family. Check your local telephone directory to see if there is an Irish American historical or genealogical society in your area.

The Irish Ancestral Research Association (TIARA)
P.O. Box 619
Sudbury, MA 01776

Irish Family History Society
P.O. Box 36
Naas
Co. Kildare, Ireland

Irish Family Names Society
P.O. Box 2095
La Mesa, CA 92044-0600

Irish Genealogical Society
P.O. Box 16069
St. Paul, MN 55116

New England Historic Genealogical Society
101 Newbury St.
Boston, MA 02116

New Jersey Historical Society
Genealogy Club of the Library
230 Broadway
Newark, NJ 07104

New York Genealogical and Biographical Society
122–126 East 58th St.
New York, NY 10022

New York Irish History Roundtable
P.O. Box 2087

Church Street Station
New York, NY 10008

RESEARCHING YOUR ROOTS IN IRELAND

Baxter, Angus. *In Search of Your British and Irish Roots*. **New York: William Morrow, 1982.**

There is a small section in this book on where to go for information in Ireland.

Betit, Kyle J., and Radford, Dwight A. *Ireland: A Genealogical Guide for North Americans*. **Salt Lake City: The Irish at Home and Abroad, 1995.**

An easy-to-understand but detailed overview of Irish record sources accessible from the United States.

Burke, Sir Bernard. *History of the Colonial Gentry*. **2 vols. London: Harris and Sons, 1891.**

If your ancestors were gentry, this is the place to go. Known as "Burke's List," this source has information on the genealogies and coats of arms of hundreds of families.

Culligan-Hogan, Matthew J. *The Quest for the Galloping Hogan*. **New York: Crown Publishers, 1979.**

An Irish American man begins a search all around Europe to find out the true story of the "Galloping Hogan," a hero of ballads and family stories. He learns that the hero was a real person and discovers much more about his family in the process.

De Breffny, Brian. *Irish Family Names: Arms, Origins and Locations*. **Dublin: Gill and Macmillan, 1982.**

Covers 1,000 family names and color pictures of coats of arms; includes some historical information.

Falley, Margaret Dickson. *Irish and Scotch-Irish Ancestral Research: A Guide to the Genealogical*

Records, Methods and Sources in Ireland. 2 vols. Baltimore: Genealogical Publishing Co., 1988 (originally published 1962).

A very thorough guide to the kinds of records and resources available in Ireland and the United States.

Fallon, John J. *A Better Deed*. New York: BBI, 1995.

Beginning with the story of his family in Ireland, Fallon changes some elements and elaborates on others to tell a compelling story of a family in Ballinlass over time.

Flanagan, Deirdre, and Flanagan, Laurence. *Irish Place Names*. Dublin: Gill and Macmillan, 1994.

Trying to figure out what those Irish place names mean in English? This book explains the origin and derivation of names in more than 3,000 cities, towns, villages, and physical features.

***General Alphabetical Index to the Townlands and Towns, Parishes and Baronies of Ireland.* Baltimore: Genealogical Publishing Co., 1995 (originally published in 1861).**

Based on the census of Ireland for 1851, this book can help you locate a town that you have only heard of.

Glazier, Ira A., ed. *The Famine Immigrants: Lists of Irish Immigrants Arriving at the Port of New York, 1846–1851*. 8 vols. Baltimore: Genealogical Publishing Co., 1985.

These eight volumes include lists of 651,931 passengers arriving from Ireland on 2,743 different voyages during this period.

Grehan, Ida. *Irish Family Histories*. Boulder, CO: Roberts Rinehart, 1995.

Covering 200 family names, divided into eighty groups. There is information on each name's origin, geographic distribution, and immigration to the United States and elsewhere. Includes notable people having each surname. Many illustrations.

Grenham, John. *Tracing Your Irish Ancestors: The Complete Guide.* **Baltimore: Genealogical Publishing Co., 1992.**

A very clear and comprehensive guide for tracing your ancestors in Ireland. Includes an excellent set of maps of all Catholic parishes, lists of resources (such as passenger and emigrant lists), publications on emigration, county-by-county source lists, and Church of Ireland record lists.

Harris, Ruth-Ann M., and Jacobs, Donald M., eds. *The Search for Missing Friends: Irish Immigrant Advertisements Placed in the* **Boston Pilot. Vol. 1: 1831–50, Vol. 2: 1851–53. Boston: New England Historic Genealogical Society, 1989.**

Many of the thousands of Irish immigrants who came to North America in the nineteenth century became "lost" to their friends or family in the United States or Ireland. Some were separated at dockside or later, while others lost touch with kin in Ireland. These books print out the ads placed in the "Missing Friends" section of a major Irish American newspaper. This information is useful for tracking down who arrived, who was considered missing, and locations of family homes in Ireland.

Helferty, Seamus, and Refausse, Raymond, eds. *Directory of Irish Archives*, **2d ed. Dublin: Irish Academic Press, 1993.**

A listing of 224 repositories and organizations that have records of historical significance, with a list of their major collections. Includes educational, religious, cultural, and government organizations.

Howard, Joseph J., and Crisp, Frederick A., eds. *Visitation of Ireland.* **Baltimore: Genealogical Publishing**

Co., 1973 (originally published in six volumes in London, 1897–1918).

A massive book listing the pedigrees of eminent Irish families, including information on crests and heralds. Not light reading, but if you are related to one of these families, there is information dating back to the seventeenth and eighteenth centuries.

Lewis, Samuel. *A Topographical Dictionary of Ireland.* **2 vols. Baltimore: Genealogical Publishing Co., 1995 (reprinted from original 1837 publication).**

A good resource to find out about the small towns, parishes, and villages of Ireland. Includes historical and statistical descriptions of the towns.

MacLysaght, Edward. *Irish Families: Their Names, Arms and Origins,* **3d ed. Dublin: Hodges Figgis, 1972.**

This is the bible for family research in Ireland. It is an excellent starting point, with lists of family names, where the family came from, who was famous in the family, and what the official coat of arms is for that family.

———. *More Irish Families.* **Dublin: O'Gorman Ltd., 1960.**

Additional families are documented in this genealogical dictionary.

———. *Supplement to Irish Families.* **Baltimore: Genealogical Book Company, 1964.**

More families included.

McCarthy, Tony. *Irish Roots Guide.* **Dublin: Lilliput, 1991.**

The objective of this guide is to assist in a "nontraditional" tracing of an entire family rather than just the male line (which was traditionally important for tracing the descent of property). After defining basic terms and issues for genealogical research, it describes twelve major documentary sources and how to use them.

Mitchell, Brian. *A Guide to Irish Parish Registers*. Baltimore: Genealogical Publishing Co., 1988.

County-by-county lists of all parish registers available, both civil and religious.

————. *A New Genealogical Atlas of Ireland*. Baltimore: Genealogical Publishing Co., 1986.

All major Irish record sources are linked to an administrative unit: county, barony, civil parish, diocese, Poor Law Union, and probate district. This is an atlas of maps of those administrative units. An excellent tool for figuring out which records you will need in your genealogical search.

O'Connor, Michael H. *A Guide to Tracing Your Kerry Ancestors*, 2d ed. Dublin: Flyleaf Press, 1994.

If your family comes from Kerry, this is a good resource. Includes lists of County Kerry family histories and publications on County Kerry itself.

O'Laughlin, Michael C. *The Complete Book for Tracing Your Irish Ancestors*. Kansas City, MO: Irish Genealogical Foundation, 1982.

An overview of the steps necessary to trace your ancestry, including lists of records available in Ireland and the United States.

————. *The Master Book of Irish Placenames*. Kansas City, MO: Irish Genealogical Foundation, 1994.

A master atlas with lists of place names (with alternative spellings), where they are located, and maps of the sites.

Ryan, James G. *A Guide to Tracing Your Dublin Ancestors*. Dublin: Flyleaf Press, 1988.

The major sources of family records for the city and county of Dublin are listed, and described with illustrated examples. Includes commercial and local directories and newspaper holdings (which provide birth, marriage, and death notices).

———. *Irish Records: Sources for Family and Local History*. Salt Lake City: Ancestry, Inc., 1988.

A thorough reference book divided into chapters on each county. Presents a brief history of the county, what records survive, and where they are located. Includes a helpful introduction that explains the value of the different sources and how to access them.

COATS OF ARMS AND HERALDRY

Fairbairn's Book of Crests of the Families of Great Britain and Ireland, 4th ed. 2 vols. London: T. C. and E. C. Jack, 1892.

This standard reference work is a massive compilation of surnames, crests, and mottoes, with a volume of coats-of-arms illustrations.

Friar, Stephen, ed. *A New Dictionary of Heraldry*. London: Alpha Books, 1987.

Heraldry began as a way of identifying knights in full armor as they paraded and fought. Heraldry continues to record family history. This is a good reference guide to the heraldic arts, including basic terminology and detailed descriptions of some elements, as well as some of the issues and debates in the field. Illustrations included.

———, and Ferguson, John. *Basic Heraldry*. New York: W. W. Norton, 1993.

This is an excellent introduction to the subject of heraldry, including its history, medieval tournaments, and the orders of chivalry. Scottish, Welsh, and Irish systems of heraldry are discussed. Using excellent drawings and illustrations, there is detailed analysis of the elements in a coat of arms.

Murtaugh, Paul. *Your Irish Coats-of-Arms*. **New York: Ainsworth Company, 1960.**

Beautiful color illustrations for over 2,000 Irish names.

Puttock, A. G. *A Dictionary of Heraldry and Related Subjects*. **New York: Arco Publishing, 1985.**

Divided into three sections: a dictionary of terms used in heraldry; terms used regarding armor and arms; and information on where to write for genealogical information in Ireland. A useful sourcebook for information on technical terms used in heraldry and arms.

JOURNALS

The Irish at Home and Abroad
P.O. Box 521806
Salt Lake City, UT 84152
801-238-2562

The Irish at Home and Abroad provides articles and information on how to conduct Irish family research in a realistic fashion. Information is geared toward both the beginner and the more advanced researcher. Specific topics such as immigration and migration patterns within the United States are also discussed.

Irish Genealogist
c/o The Irish Club
82 Eaton Square
London SW1W 9AJ, United Kingdom

Unpublished source materials, general account books, narrative pedigrees, and some Irish family histories will be found here.

Irish Roots
Belgrave Publications

Belgrave Avenue
Cork, Ireland

For the latest happenings in Irish genealogy, this publication is a must. It contains excellent articles on specific repositories and on the Heritage Centers.

Other periodicals are available depending on the area you are researching. Your librarian can help you find a list of them. You can also check the *Preci Index*, which lists and indexes many genealogical magazines.

WHERE TO PURCHASE IRISH MATERIALS

Irish Book Shop
580 Broadway, Room 1103
New York, NY 10012
212-274-1923

This shop, specializing in Irish-language materials, also has an extensive inventory of Irish and Irish American histories and biographies. It is a good place to browse.

Irish Books and Media
The Franklin Business Center
1433 Franklin Avenue East
Minneapolis, MN 55404-2135
612-871-3505
Fax: 612-871-3358

This company's catalog is extensive and covers a wide range of topics related to Ireland.

Irish Visions, Inc.
4338 Katonah Avenue
Woodlawn, NY 10470
718-325-9014

Call or write for a catalog of Irish music and documentary videos.

Chapter 5
Interviewing Your Relatives

Imagine trying to record important accomplishments and significant events in a society where there are no radios, televisions, libraries, post offices, or computers. For those of us who have come to rely on modern methods of technology and communication, this might seem an impossible task. Yet our ancestors, some of whom lacked a written language or the ability to read and write, have managed to provide us with thousands of years worth of valuable history.

The process of collecting information through personal interviews is still widely used today, and is known as oral history. In many societies around the world today, oral history is still the most common method of transmitting information from generation to generation.

Interviewing your relatives and family friends will be an important part of your genealogical search. In the 1940s, historian Allan Nevins found that people were becoming increasingly dependent on the telephone as a form of communication. He realized that because of the dependence on spoken communication, they would no longer be leaving behind the papers and letters that history thrived on. With this thought in mind, Nevins started a collection of oral history at Columbia University. He and his fellow researchers preserved autobiographical accounts of the lives of famous and prominent people through tape-recorded interviews.

Your interviewees may not be famous, but hearing them tell their own stories can make the past come alive and bring a more personal and emotional dimension to your genealogical research. Recording the experiences of your family members not only provides you with valuable information—it can

also be one of the most intriguing and enjoyable aspects of
your genealogical search.

Preparation and the Interview

It is important that you prepare yourself properly before
conducting interviews. Make sure that you have collected the
documents and written material concerning your family
before beginning the interviewing process. Having these
documents close at hand will make it easier for you to for-
mulate specific questions and may give you additional information about other friends and family members that your
interviewee might mention. After assembling your materials,
choose your interviewee or informant (the term used by oral
historians). Do not exclude older relatives you are close to
just because you feel you have heard all of the stories they
have to tell. In fact, you may wish to start with someone you
know well and gradually move on to less familiar friends and
family members as you gain more confidence and experience
with the interviewing process. You will probably find that
there are still many stories you have not heard. You can also
press for more information about a specific story, even if you
have heard it many times.

Once you have settled on an interviewee, request an ap-
pointment. It is wise to arrange the meeting well in advance
so that both of you have some time to reflect on what you
would like to ask or discuss. Do not be discouraged if a
friend or family member refuses to be interviewed. They
may feel that they have no stories that would be of interest
to younger generations. Or they may not be comfortable
talking about their lives. Take the time to explain that you
decided to research your family history because their lives
and experiences are of interest to you. The sincere interest
that you take in the life of a family member may convince
them that they do have a history worth sharing. Once a
relative or friend has agreed to be interviewed, decide on a
time and place. Since many people are hesitant about the
interviewing process, it is a good idea to hold the interview
in a place where the interviewee feels at home and comfort-

able. Wherever you choose to conduct the interview, make sure it is a place where you will be free from interruptions. Ringing phones and barking dogs can impede concentration. If the interview is to be conducted over the phone, set up a time when you and the interviewee will both be able to remove yourselves from disruptions.

Now that you have collected the appropriate materials and selected an interviewee, your next task is to prepare an interview outline and list of questions. Just as you made an effort to choose a comfortable setting for your interview, create questions that will allow your interviewee to feel confident and relaxed. The order in which you ask questions is very important. Consider leading off the interview with simple factual questions about age, place and date of birth, and religion. Even though you may be eager to hear about your grandmother's childhood in County Clare, starting an interview with questions that require her to recall the distant past may make her feel slow and discouraged. Struggling for answers is no fun. Your interviewees may need time to "jog their memory," to adjust to being recorded, or to feel comfortable with the surroundings.

Remember that you will need to ask open-ended questions rather than closed questions. Examples of open-ended questions are:

> "Do you remember your grandmother and grandfather? What were they like?"

> "How did you meet your spouse?"

> "What did the family do on vacation? Where did you go and what did you like about it?"

A closed-ended question is one for which the answer is one or two words, such as:

> "Did you like school?"

> "Where did you work?"

Sometimes the facts can come out of a closed question, but it will take more work from you. An open-ended question requires the interviewee to share more of what he or she knows.

Sample Questions
Childhood
- Where were you born and when were you baptized? Who were your godparents and what was their relationship to your parents?
- How many brothers and sisters did you have? Where are you in your family's birth order?
- What was your household like when you were a child? Did any of your grandparents ever live with you?
- How many times did you move and where did you live?
- What schools did you attend and what subjects did you like?
- How would you describe your family's financial situation?
- What were your hobbies? What did you do for fun?
- Did you go to college? Where and when? What was your major and why did you choose it?
- If you did not attend college, did you receive any training beyond high school?

Adulthood
- Where was your first job and what did you do?
- What types of jobs have you held?
- What were your hobbies?
- How, when, and where did you meet your spouse and what did you think of him/her at first?
- When and where did you get married? Who was in the wedding party? Who attended the wedding? Where was the reception?
- How many children did you have? What are their names and dates of birth?
- Where did you take your family on vacations?

In your oral history interviews, you may want to ask your relatives about their views on political issues. The Troubles in Northern Ireland have long been a major concern among Irish Americans. At a demonstration in New York City, a protester holds a cross with a photo of one of the thirteen unarmed civilians killed during the "Bloody Sunday" massacre in Derry, Northern Ireland, in 1972. The civilians were killed by the British Army in response to the deaths of forty-eight British soldiers at the hands of the Irish Republican Army.

- Did you serve in the military? If so, what branch did you serve in and what was it like?
- Have you visited Ireland? What were your impressions?

General Questions
- What are your likes and dislikes?
- What was your most exciting moment? Happiest memory? Saddest memory?
- What advice did your parents give you? Would you give the same advice to your children?

Remember to be flexible. This is a gradual process. By starting with general questions, you can lead the interviewee to more details. Do not limit your questions to the ones you have on paper, because you could miss some very important information. Jot down new questions as you think of them. As some people age, dates are not as important to them. If you are asking an aunt about her grandfather, you can start with "What do you remember about Grandfather and when did he die?" She may not remember the exact date, but she may tell you that she was in fourth grade at the time and it was just after Christmas. You have narrowed the time to December or January when she was nine or ten years old.

Do not be insulted if there are things some relatives do not wish to discuss. A divorce in a Catholic family might be regarded as something to be kept secret. Other family problems, such as being arrested or having a mental illness, may fall into this category. If your interviewee tells you that something is confidential, you must respect his or her wishes.

How do you keep track of all the information you gather? The easiest way is to record the interview with a battery-operated or electronic tape recorder. You will want to use an external microphone for two reasons. First, this allows you to put the microphone closer to the subject, and you will get a better recording. Secondly, if you use the internal microphone, the noise of the motor will also be recorded.

Using a tape recorder allows you to be more relaxed. Instead of trying to write down every word, you can pay attention to your subject. You should still take notes during the interview, however, even if you are recording it.

The newest way to record an interview is to videotape it. If you have access to the equipment and your interviewee agrees, give it a try. This works best if you sit with the subject and someone else does the taping. To prepare for this type of interview, ask your subject if there are any objects or pictures that he or she would like to capture on videotape. Pictures and mementos can relax your subject and reduce his or her nervousness.

Whether you are interviewing a person born in Ireland or New York, you will have few language problems. There may be an accent or a brogue, but by listening to the tapes you will begin to understand what they are saying. Most of your relatives will be glad to see that you are taking an interest in the family. Once you have done the first interview, do not be surprised if other relatives volunteer to be next.

Digging Deeper

There is a wide range of topics that you can focus on in an oral history interview. Some interviewers prefer to explore many topics in a single interview. Although the information you obtain will be less detailed, you will find that this option gives variety to your genealogical search. Other interviewers pick a specific topic to focus on and create a whole interview full of questions on just that subject. For example, you might consider spending one full session on the interviewee's memories of his or her education. This approach may provide you with specific information about Ireland's educational system and how it differs from schools in the United States. You may be treated to detailed remembrances of the interviewee's teachers, classmates, and schools.

If you are looking for information about specific historical events, focus on your interviewee's life experiences. Ask if they recall any major changes that took place during their lifetimes. They may recall the Great Depression or they may

Ask your relatives about organizations they or other family members belonged to, in both Ireland and the United States. The Fenians were a secret society organized to help Ireland fight for its freedom from Britain. This banner depicts the leaders of the Fenians.

have fought in a major war. Where were they and what were they doing when Irish American President John F. Kennedy was assassinated? In addition to asking about the details of each event, you may also want to know how these incidents affected your interviewee's life and how they made him or her feel.

Ask your interviewees questions specific to their Irish heritage. What traditions did they carry with them from Ireland to the United States? They may recall Irish holidays, food, stories, and folklore. My family passed down to me a recipe for Irish soda bread, as well as the steps to a few Irish dances and jigs. Questions about social life can make for interesting conversation. It is exciting to hear your interviewee's memories of dating, music, dances, sports, and community. You may want to ask your relatives if they belonged to any Irish organizations. Irish cultural organizations such as the Ancient Order of Hibernians have played a great role in the lives of many Irish Americans. My mother's involvement in my community's Irish Benevolent Society allowed me to take part in St. Patrick's Day festivities and meet other Irish Americans and Irish immigrants.

Questions about occupations and careers can provide you with an enormous amount of information. Since many Irish immigrants came to the United States looking for freedom, they eagerly became involved in what has historically been a symbol of democracy and American ideals: the labor union. My investigation into this topic led me to a book about my great-great-grandfather's involvement in the hatter's union. This particular labor union was an association of workers in the hat-making industry who worked together to promote and protect the welfare, rights, and interests of its members. Given to me by an interviewee, the book explained my great-great-grandfather's journey to the United States and then went on to describe his years of service to the union.

Interviewing Through the Mail

If you would like to interview a friend or relative who is far away, communicating by mail is an easy and inexpensive

Irish Americans were heavily involved in the formation of labor unions in the late nineteenth century. Above, women delegates to the 1886 convention of the Knights of Labor pose for a portrait.

alternative to speaking with an individual face to face. Begin by preparing an initial letter. Start the letter with a concise outline of the research that you have already done. This will help to pique the interest of your prospective interviewee. Inform your friend or relative that you would like to make their life experience part of your genealogical research and that you will be mailing them a questionnaire in a few days. There is no need to wait for the person to accept the interview. If you ask the person to respond to you with a "yes" or "no" answer, you could be waiting for days.

No one is *required* to answer your questions, but urge prospective interviewees to participate in your project. Mention some of the topics that you have included in the questionnaire. This will give your interviewees a chance to think about some of the important events and aspects of their lives that might pertain to your research. Allowing them to prepare will help them to respond to your questions in a more timely fashion. Finally, thank your prospective interviewees and make sure they know that you are eager to hear from them.

Your next step is to prepare a questionnaire. Layout and design are crucial factors to consider when you are creating anything on paper. The questions should be clear and easy to read. Remember that you will not be present to answer any questions that your friends or relatives might have. Think about whether you would like to have your interviewees answer the questions on a separate sheet of paper or below the actual questions. Make sure you supply interviewees with everything they need. Include additional sheets of paper and a self-addressed, stamped envelope so that interviewees can easily drop their responses in the mail to you free of charge. Always keep copies of your correspondence. This will help you to keep better track of your contacts and provide you with a reference should you decide to conduct additional interviews through the mail.

Whether you interview someone face to face or through the mail, it is imperative that you thank them. The best way to do this is through a thank-you letter shortly after the interview takes place. If interviewees are interested in knowing more about your research, explain that you will share your genealogical findings with them once you have organized your interviews, documents, and photos into a cohesive, finished product.

If there is a relative you would like to interview who lives across the country, you may want to contact him or her by using electronic mail (e-mail). If you have access to a computer with a modem or computer service such as Prodigy, America Online, or CompuServe, this can be a fast and easy way to get in touch with a relative. Much of the time, an e-mail message is faster and less expensive than a long-distance telephone call. You can also print out a hard copy of the "conversation"—much easier than transcribing a tape!

Try to learn from the previous experience of other writers and interviewers. When reading the biographies of famous individuals, try to envision what questions an interviewer may have posed to them. How would they phrase the question? What did the interviewer want to learn about this person?

The genealogical facts you can get from written sources such as books, census documents, parish records, and birth certificates are very important, but only a real, live person can tell you what it was like to sit around the turf-fire in their family's thatched-roof cottage. There are a variety of ways to approach an oral history interview and a great number of issues to consider. It may take a while to complete interviews, do additional research, and assemble all of your notes and recordings into a finished product, but the result is exciting information that you can treasure forever.

Resources

ORAL HISTORY

Alessi, Jean, and Miller, Jan. *Once Upon a Memory: Your Family Tales and Treasures.* White Hall, VA: Betterway Publications, 1987.

A general guide to recording your family history through interviewing and finding household items, such as photographs and personal records.

Allen, Barbara, and Montell, William Lynwood. *From Memory to History: Using Oral Sources in Local Historical Research.* Nashville, TN: American Association for State and Local History, 1981.

A particularly helpful guide for those wishing to use oral history material for writing a family history. Also discusses how to obtain oral history sources.

Arthur, Stephen, and Arthur, Julia. *Your Life & Times: How to Put a Life Story on Tape.* Baltimore: Genealogical Publishing Co., 1987.

Provides you with a list of questions that will lead you through your personal history. Includes advice on how to record an oral history.

Bannister, Shala Mills. *Family Treasures: Videotaping Your Family's History. A Guide for Preserving Your Family's Living History as an Heirloom for Future Generations.* Baltimore: Clearfield Co., 1994.

A guide to videotaping your family history, with advice on interviewing as well as videotaping.

Brown, Cynthia Stokes. *Like It Was: A Complete Guide to Writing Oral History.* New York: Teachers and Writers Collaborative, 1988.

A user-friendly guide to planning, interviewing, transcribing, writing, and publishing for oral historians.

Fletcher, William P. *Record Your Family History*. Berkeley, CA: Ten Speed Press, 1989.

Explains how to preserve your family's oral history on videotape and audiotape. It suggests interview techniques, includes sample questions, and gives examples of what to listen for when interviewing.

Gluck, Sherna Berger, and Patai, Daphne, eds. *Women's Words: The Feminist Practice of Oral History*. New York: Routledge, 1991.

The authors discuss issues specific to women's oral history. Consult this book for insight before interviewing female relatives.

McLaughlin, Paul. *A Family Remembers*. North Vancouver, BC: Self-Counsel Press, 1993.

A fine guide to creating a family history with video cameras and tape recorders. Includes tips on lighting, acoustics, interviewing, and editing.

Shumway, Gary L., and Hartley, William G. *An Oral History Primer*. Salt Lake City: Shumway, 1973.

The authors explain the significance of oral history to family heritage. They also tell you what to do with tales and songs once you have recorded them.

Thompson, Paul. *The Voice of the Past: Oral History*. New York: Oxford University Press, 1978.

A description of oral history, its uses, and how to document it. See especially the list of sample questions.

INTERVIEWING

Banaka, William H. *Training in Depth Interviewing*. New York: Harper & Row, 1971.

Helps you keep your interviews organized and focused. Includes tips on preparation, effective questions to ask, and strategies for getting the information you want from the interviewee.

Davis, Cullom; Back, Kathryn; and Maclean, Kay. *Oral History: From Tape to Type.* **Chicago: American Library Association, 1977.**

Contains information on interviewing, transcribing, and editing oral history data. Also gives helpful tips on note-taking and organization of interviews.

Deering, Mary Jo, and Pomeroy, Barbara. *Transcribing Without Tears: A Guide to Transcribing and Editing Oral History Interviews.* **Washington, DC: Oral History Program, George Washington University Library, 1976.**

What do you do now that you have a collection of taped interviews with family members? This book will guide you through the difficult but important process of transcribing your tapes. It also shows you what to do with tricky situations such as an interviewee who rambles or speaks unclearly.

Evans, George Ewart. *Spoken History.* **London: Faber and Faber, 1987.**

See chapter 2, "The Interview," for advice on interviewing with tape recorders.

Harvey, Joanne H. *The Living Record: Interviewing and Other Techniques for Genealogists.* **Lansing, MI: J. H. Harvey, 1985.**

This book is geared specifically to genealogists. It provides tips on interviewing and on incorporating oral history into a family history.

Jenkins, Sara, ed. *Past, Present: Recording Life Stories of Older People.* **Washington, DC: St. Albans Parish, 1978.**

This "how-to" manual can be ordered from the publications department of the National Council on Aging, 409 Third Street, SW, Washington, DC 20024.

Payne, Stanley L. *The Art of Asking Questions.* **Princeton, NJ: Princeton University Press, 1951.**

This book, though old, still provides useful information on how to ask questions in an interview, including suggestions on how to word questions.

Schumacher, Michael. *Creative Conversations: The Writer's Guide to Conducting Interviews.* **Cincinnati: Writer's Digest, 1990.**

This is a guide to interviewing for all kinds of writers. Find out how to ask questions to get the information you need while at the same time leaving room for your interviewee to open up and surprise you with new information.

Stano, Michael E., and Reinsch, Jr., N. L. *Communication in Interviews.* **Englewood Cliffs, NJ: Prentice-Hall, 1982.**

Although this is a general interviewing text, its concepts can be easily applied to a genealogical interview. Topics discussed include preparation, strategies for communicating clearly, and reading verbal and nonverbal signals.

Chapter 6
Putting It All Together

You have been working diligently on your family history, but now you have hit a roadblock. The records just do not seem to be there. You have mounds of papers and tapes of interviews. What do you do now?

This is the time to start pulling things together. You may want to use a computer program like Family Tree Maker or Personal Ancestral File. These programs can help you to organize and present your findings. As you input the names and dates into your computer files, you may see something you missed the first time. You may want to reexamine some of your earliest work.

Writing a family history can be a labor of love. It will be something that not only you and your immediate family will treasure, but also your relatives on both sides of the family and future generations.

There are many ways for you to present your genealogical findings. In fact, the only limit is your own imagination. But there are some standard formats that genealogists use to share their findings with others.

Family Trees

Almost everyone has had to create some sort of family tree at one point in their lives. Whether they are simple grade-school assignments or the work of a professional genealogist, all family trees follow some fundamental rules. For example, all family trees start with one ancestor and work their way forward to the present. This is the reverse of the pedigree charts, which begin with you and trace your roots *back* through time.

Therefore, as a starting point for your family tree, you should choose an ancestor who lived as far back in history as possible. This ancestor will represent the trunk of your family tree. The family tree should trace only this bloodline. Branching out from him or her will be the children, then grandchildren, great-grandchildren, continuing up to the present. You will see the tree begin to branch out as more and more generations are added to it. If your family tree goes all the way to the present, you will be one of the highest, if not the highest, branch on the tree.

You should be able to get all of the information you need from your boxes and binders of findings. Use the pedigree charts and family group sheets as chronological and factual reference points to check against. You can use your other data to fill in the essential information about each person: name, birth date and place, marriage date (if married), date of death, and place of burial. You will find that all good family trees contain this information.

If you were unable to gather some piece of information about one or more of your relatives, do not worry. All you need to do is leave those spaces blank on the family tree and fill them in when you do find the relevant information. Likewise, leave spaces for any relatives you are missing. Hopefully, you will be able to complete the entire tree someday, but do not trouble yourself too much if you cannot. Even some of the most detailed family trees lack information of some kind.

As for the decoration and illustration of your family tree, it can be as simple or as elaborate as you like. The tree might consist of some lines you have drawn on a piece of paper. On the other hand, you could draw or paint a beautiful tree to frame and hang on your wall. Some people even get their family trees professionally illustrated or painted, although this can be expensive.

You can also include photographs of your ancestors on the tree. This is a wonderful way to bring the information to life for others to enjoy. It will also allow you to see what kinds of physical features—curly hair, freckles, or deep-set eyes, for example—have been passed on through the generations. Since you will not want to cut and paste your irreplaceable family photographs, you can photocopy them instead. Cut each photocopied picture into a square, circle, or some other uniform shape and attach it to the tree above the person's name. These portraits will add an exciting dimension to your family tree.

Writing a Family History

Another way to gather your information into a coherent whole is to write a family history. Like the family tree, your writing can take on any number of forms. If you are very serious about your family history and hope to someday have it published, you must give sources for all the information you include. Or you might choose to gather a collection of entertaining family lore in which you would have to cite relatively few records beyond the names of relatives quoted and the date of the quote. While there is plenty of room for creativity, there are a number of rules that written family histories usually follow.

Primarily, a family history should be a narrative presentation of the genealogical data you have collected. In other words, your historical information should read as smoothly as a story. Also, your history, like the pedigree chart, should begin with information about yourself and reach back into your family's past. Since you want your family history to be clear and enjoyable to read, you should focus on one family line. If you try to include every piece of material from your search, you could end up with a story that is 1,000 pages long—far too long for all but the most dedicated to enjoy.

Do not hesitate to include any photographs or other visual memorabilia you have collected. Pictures of relatives will make the story of your family come alive. You could also include photographs of family heirlooms or homes where family members have lived. As with your family tree, you may want to make photocopies of the pictures in your history so that you do not ruin an irreplaceable family treasure.

The more interesting the format you use, the more people will be interested in reading it. Maybe you want to start a family newsletter that contains information from your genealogical project. This would be a great way to keep the lines of communication open between you and your family members, and it could provide you with helpful responses as you continue your search. You may have audio or video recordings from your interviews with relatives. These can be used to create an audio or visual presentation of your family history.

Writing an Autobiography

By now you know as well as anyone how difficult it is to gather genealogical information. Any help you received, whether it was from a librarian, another genealogical researcher, or a helpful book, was greatly appreciated. Imagine how much easier your work would have been if one of the subjects of your research had written a book about herself and her immediate family. If you could have found such a resource, you no doubt would have been very thankful.

Writing your autobiography can be your contribution to the world of genealogical research. You may think that such a venture is tooting your own horn, but nothing could be further from the truth. There are two important reasons why writing an autobiography is not simply self-serving. First of all, as mentioned earlier, your writings will be invaluable to future genealogical researchers in your family. Second, your autobiography will not contain information only about you.

Your life has been influenced by many other people, most importantly your parents, siblings, and other family members. As a result, you should include a bit about your parents in your autobiography—when and where they were born and married, and when and where they had their children. Mention some things about your brothers, sisters, aunts, uncles, cousins, and grandparents. Write about how these people affected your life. Surely your parents' jobs and social lives, for example, have influenced your own life.

Do not hesitate to include any piece of information about your own life. Write about your everyday life in your home and in your town. Write about classes you took at school, your first jobs, and even your favorite pastimes. Tell about your family pets, family trips, and family gatherings. Finally, talk about your life today. You can include items from your genealogical search, such as photographs of relatives, photos of family heirlooms, and a copy of your family tree. This kind of data is just another aspect of what has made you into the person you are today. And chances are, if such information concerning other peoples' lives was helpful or interesting to you during your search, it will be helpful or interesting to researchers in the future.

Computer Genealogy

Genealogical research has traditionally been recorded either orally or in writing. But don't forget that we have entered the computer age. Like many other endeavors, genealogy has benefitted from the computer. There are a variety of software programs that have been created especially for genealogists to store what they find.

The most popular, and one of the best, software programs for genealogical research has been created by the Church of Jesus Christ of Latter-day Saints. Their computer program, the Personal Ancestral File (PAF), is a database that allows you to record, sort, print, and transmit your genealogical gatherings with your computer. The program is fairly easy to use for anyone with basic computer skills, and it is relatively inexpensive to purchase. It may save you time in recording and accessing information, as well as saving space. Although you will probably still want to keep a hard copy of everything in your folders and boxes, the amount of paper used will be considerably reduced because your information can be stored on disk.

The PAF program, and other programs like it, also allow you to print out your genealogical information in a number of different forms. If you are not artistically inclined, or just do not feel like drawing a family tree, these programs will usually do a nice job for you. If you use a genealogical program in conjunction with one of the many desktop publishing programs that are on the market, you could end up with a beautifully organized end result.

Irish Arts and Traditions

Irish traditions may have been passed down in your family for many generations. Or, you may be forging new ground as the first person in your family in many years to show a deep interest in your Irish heritage. Whatever your own situation, you may want to learn more about the arts, music, foods, and crafts of your ancestral land. In many cities, there are Irish cultural organizations, and some of these offer workshops and classes in traditional Irish crafts and music. If there is not such an organization near you, you can learn more on your own by looking at some of the books listed in the **Resources**.

Your exploration into the world of Irish traditions can be incorporated into your genealogical project. Include a soda bread recipe or the lyrics of a traditional Irish song in your written family history. If you have the chance to present your project at a family reunion, this might be an opportunity to lead the family in singing or dancing in traditional Irish fashion. If you put together an audiotape or videotape with the results of your research, you can include the sound of yourself playing a traditional Irish musical instrument as background music.

Good Luck!

Now it is up to you. You are equipped with the knowledge to document successfully your family history. One last thing for you to remember is: Enjoy yourself. No matter how important your genealogy is to you and your family, it is just a hobby. So work hard and have fun, and your exploration will be a truly gratifying experience. Best of luck!

> *May the road rise to meet you. May the wind always be at your back, the sun shine warm upon your face, the rain fall soft upon your fields, and until we meet again may God hold you in the hollow of his hand.*
>
> —Traditional Irish Toast

Resources

WRITING YOUR FAMILY HISTORY

Barnes, Donald R., and Lackey, Richard S. *Write It Right: A Manual for Writing Family Histories and Genealogies.* **Ocala, FL: Lyon Press, 1983.**

> Considered a must-have book by genealogists, this volume tells readers how to preserve their precious family facts and memories for future generations to read.

The Chicago Manual of Style: The Essential Guide for Writers, Editors, and Publishers, **14th ed. Chicago: University of Chicago Press, 1993.**

> An authoritative and comprehensive reference guide for anyone who works with words, be it for scholastic or professional purposes. This manual contains answers to many questions regarding style, grammar, and usage in the English language.

Costello, Margaret F., and Fiske, Jane Fletcher. *Guidelines for Genealogical Writing.* **Bowie, MD: Heritage Books, 1988.**

> Suggestions on style for genealogical writers.

Gouldrup, Lawrence P. *Writing the Family Narrative.* **Salt Lake City: Ancestry, Inc., 1987.**

> If you want to compile your research into book form, consult this volume for guidance.

Jordan, Lewis. *Cite Your Sources: A Manual for Documenting Family Histories and Genealogical Records.* **Jackson: University Press of Mississippi, 1980.**

> Citing your sources ensures accuracy in your genealogical

project. This book gives advice on how to make citations clear for a variety of genealogical sources.

ILLUSTRATING YOUR FAMILY HISTORY

Earnest, Russell D. *Grandma's Attic: Making Heirlooms Part of Your Family History*. **Albuquerque, NM: R. D. Earnest Assoc., 1991.**

This book tells you what you should look for besides letters and diaries when exploring the family storage area.

Frisch-Ripley, Karen. *Unlocking Secrets in Old Photos*. **Salt Lake City: Ancestry, Inc., 1991.**

Explains how to date photos, identify faces in pictures, and restore old photos. Also includes uses for photos in a family tree or other genealogical presentations.

Time-Life Books. *Caring for Photographs*. **New York: Time-Life Books, 1973.**

A handy guide to storing, displaying, and restoring old photographs and prints.

Weinstein, Robert A., and Booth, Larry. *Collection, Use and Care of Historical Photographs*. **Nashville, TN: American Association for State and Local History, 1977.**

An excellent guide for presenting and preserving historic photographs. Also includes a history of photographic methods from 1839.

AUTOBIOGRAPHY

Daniel, Lois. *How to Write Your Own Life Story*. **Chicago: Review Press, 1980.**

A practical guide to writing autobiography.

Hoffman, William. *Life Writing: A Guide to Family Journals and Personal Memoirs*. **New York: St. Martin's Press, 1982.**

With an emphasis on capturing details about family and self, Hoffman provides guidance on recording life's ups and downs in writing.

Ledoux, Denis. *Turning Memories into Memoirs: A Handbook for Writing Lifestories*. Lisbon Falls, ME: Soleil Press, 1993.

This book will help you to record your own life story as well as those of family members. Includes examples of writing by students who have attended the author's workshops as well as specific tips on how to get your ideas flowing and your pen moving. The chapter on interviewing and research is focused on conducting interviews to jar your own memories, but will also be useful for conducting oral history interviews.

Nicols, Evelyn, and Lowenkopf, Anne. *Lifelines: A Guide to Writing Your Personal Recollections*. Crozet, VA: Betterway Publications, 1989.

The authors discuss how to make interesting reading of your musings and memories.

Thomas, Frank. *How to Write the Story of Your Life*. Cincinnati: Writer's Digest Books, 1984.

A basic guide to gathering your recollections of experiences into a coherent body of writing.

Weitzman, David, *My Backyard History Book*. Boston: Little, Brown, 1975.

Geared especially to young readers, showing them how history can be found even in their own backyards.

GENEALOGICAL SOFTWARE

American Genealogical Lending Library
P.O. Box 244
Bountiful, UT 84010
801-295-5446

Holdings include electronic databases that can be accessed by telephone, census records on CD-ROM, and marriage records on diskette.

Ancestral File Operations Unit
50 East North Temple Street
Salt Lake City, UT 84150
801-240-2584

Write for information on the Personal Ancestral File from the Family History Library.

Banner Blue Software
P.O. Box 7865
Fremont, CA 94537
510-795-4490

Write or call for information on the Biography Maker software program. This program allows you to write one ancestor's story at a time and to tie several stories together with writing and history aids.

Clifford, Karen. *Genealogy and Computers for the Complete Beginner: A Step-by-Step Guide to the PAF Computer Program, Automated Data Bases, Family History Centers, and Local Sources.* **Baltimore: Clearfield Company, 1995.**

Allows you to utilize the enormous resources of the Church of Jesus Christ of Latter-day Saints through the Personal Ancestral File. Explains how to obtain records from the LDS Family History Centers.

Commsoft, Inc.
7795 Bell Road
P.O. Box 310
Windsor, CA 95495-0130

Write for information on their Roots IV software program, which allows for different approaches to data entry.

Dollarhide Systems
203 Holly Street

Bellingham, WA 28225
801-298-5358

> Write or call for information on their Everyone's Family Tree software, which is easy for beginners to learn.

IRISH ARTS AND TRADITIONS ˙

Bain, George. *Celtic Art: The Methods of Construction*. **New York: Dover, 1973.**

> If you want a sampling of Celtic patterns and designs, this completely illustrated book will appeal, with everything from spiral patterns to Celtic lettering from the *Book of Kells*.

Bence-Jones, Mark. *A Guide to Irish Country Houses*, **rev. ed. London: Constable, 1988.**

> A reference book that includes descriptions of approximately 2,000 Irish country houses, with information on the history and ownership of the houses as well as other related information. This book will be of special interest to anyone researching architecture.

Canainn, Tomas O. *Traditional Music in Ireland*. **Loudon, NH: Ossian Publications, 1993.**

> Discusses the structure and style of traditional Irish music. Describes features of old-style singing, and presents a survey of those who collected traditional music. Includes many examples of translations of texts from the Gaelic.

Cirker, Blanche, ed. *The Book of Kells: Selected Plates in Full Color*. **New York: Dover, 1982.**

> The *Book of Kells*, containing four gospels and other religious material, was calligraphed and illuminated in approximately 800 AD. These thirty-two full-color plates provide a good view of this work.

Cole, Rosalind. *Of Soda Bread and Guinness*. **New York: RPC International Publications, Ltd., 1988.**

A cookbook combined with a portrait of Ireland depicted in terms of its people, places, traditions, and cooking lore. Pictures and stories of places and food.

Connery, Clare. *In an Irish Country Kitchen*. New York: Simon and Schuster, 1992.

With lavish color photos of both food and countryside, this book provides many recipes and stories of the culinary traditions of the Irish.

De Breffny, Brian. *Castles of Ireland*. New York: Thames and Hudson, 1977.

This book contains lots of photographs of these incredible monuments from another era.

Fitzgibbon, Theodora. *Irish Traditional Food*. Dublin: Gill and Macmillan, 1991.

Besides recipes, you get a taste of the history and social traditions of Ireland. Includes recipes from the sixteenth to twentieth centuries, from town and country, rich and poor.

Harbison, Peter; Potterton, Homan; and Sheehy, Jeanne. *Irish Art and Architecture from Prehistory to the Present*. New York: Thames and Hudson, 1993.

This richly illustrated work traces trends in art and architecture, and the historical influences on these arts in Ireland.

Hollingworth, Shelagh. *The Complete Book of Traditional Aran Knitting*. New York: St. Martin's Press, 1982.

The Aran Islands, off the west coast of Ireland, have been famous for their sweaters for centuries. The instructions here will help you to create your own version.

***Irish Women Artists: From the Eighteenth Century to the Present Day*. Dublin: National Gallery of Ireland and the Douglas Hyde Gallery, 1987.**

Based on an exhibit in Ireland, this book, with photographs, is a good overview of Irish women artists. Included are short essays on related topics and a dictionary of Irish women artists.

Kelly, Tom (photos), and Somerville-Large, Peter (text). *Legendary Ireland.* **Boulder, CO: Roberts Rinehart, 1995.**

This team of photographer and writer portray Ireland's historic traditions and ancient legends through a visit to Irish historical sites, monuments, and landscapes. Over 100 color photographs.

—— (photos); Somerville-Large, Peter (text); and Heaney, Seamus (poetry). *Ireland: The Living Landscape.* **Boulder, CO: Roberts Rinehart, 1992.**

This vivid book, with 120 color photographs, text, and poetry, captures the feeling of Ireland; it will make you want to visit the country.

Kennedy, Brian P. *Irish Painting.* **Boulder, CO: Roberts Rinehart, 1995.**

This beautifully visual book presents the best of Irish paintings over the past four centuries. An introduction discusses the history of Irish art, and each artist represented in the book is briefly discussed. Many large reproductions of paintings as well as many detailed photos.

Meehan, Aidan.

Celtic Design: Knotwork, 1991.
Celtic Design: A Beginner's Manual, 1991.
Celtic Design: Illuminated Letters, 1992.
Celtic Design: Animal Patterns, 1992.
Celtic Design: Spiral Patterns, 1993.
Celtic Design: Maze Patterns, 1993.

Meehan is the author of a series of well-illustrated books published by Thames and Hudson (New York) on Celtic design patterns. Each book also provides explanations and background.

Pfeiffer, Walter, and Shaffrey, Maura. *Irish Cottages.* **London: Weidenfeld and Nicolson, 1990.**

These simple cottage structures are captured in beautiful color photographs that express a sense of the country.

Shaw-Smith, David, ed. *Ireland's Traditional Crafts.* **New York: Thames and Hudson, 1984.**

The author traveled around Ireland to capture traditional crafts in their natural surroundings. With 440 illustrations of people working their crafts, he looks at textiles, stonework, woodwork, willow, leather, metalwork, pottery, glassware, and more.

Walsh, Helen. *Irish Country Cooking.* **New York: Crescent Books, 1993.**

A selection of authentic Irish recipes along with luxurious color photos of the country and the food. Captures the flavor of the land.

Weiss, Rita, ed. *Favorite Irish Crochet Designs.* **New York: Dover, 1985.**

Irish crochet, known for raised floral motifs and intricate background patterns, probably originated in the convents of Ireland. This guide instructs you in how to produce traditional Irish crochet patterns.

Glossary

agrarian   A system based on agriculture; farm-based.

ards   Plows used by the Celts to assist in farming; adapted from their iron weaponry.

bard   A poet or singer; someone who records events, stories, or interesting tales about heroic people in verse or song.

Brehons   In Celtic society, a group of attorneys who established the law of the land and maintained a lawful society without the use of police.

brogue   Term often used to describe an Irish accent.

Celts   Early Indo-European peoples; they used iron weapons when conquering Ireland in about 700 BC.

Church of Ireland   The Anglican (Protestant) church of both the Republic of Ireland and Northern Ireland.

deed   A written record of a land purchase.

documentation   Official papers and other records that verify someone's birth, marriage, death, or other information.

Druids   In Celtic society, pagan priests who schooled others before the beginning of Christianity.

Easter Rebellion   An uprising that occurred on Easter Monday in 1916, when an intense effort was made to disrupt communications and declare Ireland independent of Britain.

ethnic tourism   Travel to one's ancestral homeland to discover one's roots.

family group sheets   Forms that allow the genealogist to record historical information on each family.

feudal system   Early English system of government in which all land belonged to the king, who could grant ownership of various lands to others as he wished; in turn, landlords could divide their lands in a similar fashion.

Filidh   In Celtic society, a group of bards who maintained the history, stories, and genealogy of the people through poetry, song, and other forms of oral history.

grantor/grantee   Used on legal documents; the grantor is someone who sells the land; the grantee is someone who buys the land.

Great Famine   Also known as the Great Hunger; began in 1845 when a blight devastated Ireland's potato crop and caused many to perish from starvation.

hedge row schools   Small country schools, often outdoors, where Catholic children gathered to learn from the priests; these children were not allowed to attend other schools because of their religion.

informant   In genealogy, someone you interview to gain information about your ancestry.

mass rocks   Areas in the Irish countryside where Catholics gathered to attend mass in secret; used while the Penal Laws were in effect.

monastery   Place where religious men, such as priests or monks, live, learn, and teach.

Normans   Descendants of Vikings who settled in France in the ninth century. They conquered England in 1066 and Ireland in 1171.

oral history   Stories, poems, songs, and other information that are verbally passed down from one generation to another.

pedigree charts   Forms that allow the genealogist to record an individual's lineage.

Penal Laws   Beginning in seventeenth-century Ireland, laws created to punish people for keeping their Roman Catholic faith rather than converting to Protestantism.

plantation   In Irish society, the settling of a large tract of land by strangers.

refectory   A dining hall, like those found in monasteries.

ri   Celtic word for king; high kings were also called ard-ri.

Scotch Irish   Ethnic designation used to distinguish Irish immigrants of Protestant descent from those of

Catholic backgrounds. The Scotch Irish were the descendants of Scottish immigrants to Ireland in the seventeenth century.

The Troubles Term used to describe the fighting that has occurred between Ireland and Britain throughout Ireland's turbulent history.

vital records Official documents that record significant dates such as birth, death, and marriage.

workhouses Facilities intended to help the poor by providing work; they proved unsuccessful in Ireland's agrarian-based economy.

Index

ABOUT THE AUTHOR
Erin McKenna is a graphic designer and free-lance writer. Her ancestors immigrated to New York from County Clare and County Armagh in the nineteenth century. She lives in Chicago.

ILLUSTRATION CREDITS
Cover, © Elyse Lewin/The Image Bank; cover inset, courtesy of Vickie Gurule McSharry. Pp. viii, 9, 12, 14, 19, 21, 23, 25, 27, 29, 32, 35, 84, 86, 107, 110, 115, 135, 138, 140, BETTMANN. *Color insert:* p. 2, Official White House Photo; pp. 3, 8, AP/Wide World Photos; p. 4, © David W. Hamilton/The Image Bank; p. 5, © Bord Failte Photo; p. 6, © Gary Crallé/The Image Bank; pp. 7, 9, 13, BETTMANN; p. 10, © Michael Le Poer Trench; p. 11, © Anton Corbijn; p. 12, courtesy of Stan Rosenfield Public Relations; p. 14, © Carol Rosegg; pp. 15, 16, © Eamonn Farrell/Photocall.

LAYOUT AND DESIGN
Kim Sonsky

ACKNOWLEDGEMENTS
Many thanks to James Pomager and Patricia Little Taylor for additional research, writing, and editing.

NEW HANOVER COUNTY PUBLIC LIB

3 4200 00428504

DISCARDED
from
New Hanover County Public Library

1/97

NEW HANOVER COUNTY PUBLIC LIBRARY
201 Chestnut Street
Wilmington, N.C. 28401

GAYLORD S